ROOT & LEAF

BIG, BOLD VEGETARIAN FOOD

RICH HARRIS

PHOTOGRAPHY BY MARTIN POOLE

Kyle Books

An Hachette Company
www.hachette.co.uk

First published in Great Britain
in 2018 by Kyle Books, an imprint
of Kyle Cathie Ltd
Carmelite House,
50 Victoria Embankment
London EC4Y 0DZ
www.kylebooks.co.uk

Distributed in the US by Hachette Book Group,
1290 Avenue of the Americas,
4th and 5th Floors, New York, NY 10104

Distributed in Canada by Canadian Manda
Group, 664 Annette St., Toronto, Ontario,
Canada M6S 2C8

10 9 8 7 6 5 4 3 2 1

ISBN: 978 0 85783 441 6

Editors: Vicky Orchard, Isabel Gonzalez-
Prendergast and Judith Hannam
Design and illustrations: Sarah Greeno
sarahgreeno.com limitededitiondesign.co.uk
Photography: Martin Poole
Food styling: Rich Harris
Props styling: Polly Webb-Wilson
Production: Nic Jones and Gemma John

A Cataloguing in Publication record for this title
is available from the British Library

Printed in China

To Holly, Sebastian & Rafferty. You guys.

I'm immensely proud of this book, but none of it would be possible without the hard work and support of so many people.

Firstly to Kyle, for saying yes to this book and for your encouragement and gentle nudges in the right direction. I hope you enjoy leafing through these pages.

Martin, for turning my ideas into works of art. The fact that a dedicated carnivore such as you got excited about my recipes was so encouraging. Thanks for making every shoot day a riot, for devouring my food (and not just out of politeness), and for finally embracing the joys of coffee.

Sophie, for all of your hard work on the images and not rolling your eyes every time I said 'let's just fix it in post'. Also thanks for keeping us jacked up on caffeine and for putting up with my endless terrible jokes.

Polly, for turning my recipes into things of beauty with your stunning prop styling, advice and unrivalled eye for detail. Nobody does it better.

Pippa, Alex and Leonie, for your hard work on the shoot days, for keeping me on task throughout, and for exquisite hand modelling.

Sarah Greeno, for your beautiful design and stunning illustration.

Vicky, Judith, and Isabel at Kyle Books for turning my mad jumble of ideas into a coherent, structured book. Thank you for your patience and for allowing my deadlines to be slightly more 'elastic' than usual. Oh and Isabel, sorry we made you drink tequila on the shoot day at Borough Market.

Annie, my fantastic agent, for creating opportunities which allow me to follow my passion. Thanks for always pushing me in the right direction, fighting my corner and just generally being the nicest agent in the business. Fact.

My big brother, Simon, for the numerous trips to New York and letting me drag you to all of the restaurants, delis, bars and markets in the name of research. And my little sister, Sarah, for always being a willing taste-tester of recipes (particularly in the trial stages!).

Mum & Dad, for always having time for me and supporting me. It's been a tough year but you always come out fighting; your strength and resilience is something I can only aspire to.

Granny, whilst I'll forever be sad that you won't read this book, I'll be eternally grateful for your encouragement, wicked sense of humour and inspiration. Sorry for buggering around with your soup recipe.

Holly, my incredible wife, I love you. Thank you for your unwavering support, and for encouraging me to 'just make it bloody delicious'. Thank you for being an amazing mum to our two loons and giving me the time and space to write this book.

Sebastian and Rafferty, my boys. You make me laugh every day and I love you. Forever.

Contents

Introduction

I should begin with a disclaimer: I'm not a vegetarian. I'm a huge fan of meat and fish, but there's something exciting and challenging about pushing them to one side and focusing on vegetables as the star of the show. If we listened to every bit of dietary advice available we might not eat anything at all, such is the current climate of endless experts giving their opinions (and, more dangerously, the so-called experts amongst the clean eating brigade). However, one thing is clear, we should all be eating more vegetables and cutting back on meat and fish. I'm not going to make any health claims or offer any dietary advice, but surely eating more of the stuff that grows in the ground can only be a good thing. Without really realising it, we've cut back to only having meat a couple of times a week in our house and I think that our bodies and our wallets are beginning to thank us for it.

That said, this is not intended to be a healthy eating book. Just because the recipes are based on vegetables doesn't mean they can't occasionally be indulgent or that they'll all lead you down a virtuous path. You need only look at the Gnocchi with Caponata and Burrata Cream (page 89) or Celeriac Rice Pudding with Bramble Compote (page 194) to see that this book is all about flavour and the unadulterated joy of eating.

So whether you're a vegetarian, pescatarian or flexitarian, I want you to thumb through these pages and get excited about cooking with vegetables and the endless variety of flavours and textures that we have at our disposal if we make them the main event. I never thought I'd see myself getting genuinely excited about cooking solely with vegetables, but through the process of writing this book I've done exactly that. I'm not a strict vegetarian so didn't want to include any 'meat replacement' recipes such as veggie burgers or meat-free lasagne. There's nothing wrong with those

types of dishes, just that I've written this from the point of view of someone who will happily eat a meat-based version and relished the challenge of coming up with new ideas. However, I'm very aware that families often have a mix of vegetarians and non-vegetarians or that people can be catering for a crowd and trying to please numerous tastes. With that in mind, I've designed the recipes in the Mains chapter first and foremost as standalone dishes, but also as recipes that would work as substantial side dishes as part of a non-vegetarian meal.

The range of fruit and vegetables out there is staggering and is constantly increasing as farmers and specialist growers find ways of cultivating exotic new varieties and reviving long-forgotten crops. Even over the course of writing this book, I've made countless discoveries: lemon cucumbers, watermelon radishes, red hispi cabbage, white Russian kale and a plethora of previously unseen pumpkins. As tempting as it was to create recipes based around these new finds, I knew it would make

them inaccessible unless you happen to live within easy reach of a specialist greengrocer. I've tried to use more readily available varieties of fruit and vegetables throughout the book to encourage you to elevate the ordinary rather than grapple with the exotic. If, however, you spot an interesting looking squash, tiger-striped aubergine or violet cauliflower, then I'd encourage you use them in the recipes in place of their common counterparts. Variety is the spice of life and all that.

This leads me nicely on to how to buy vegetables. After years of trawling markets, wholesalers and specialist suppliers, I've picked up a few tips along the way; apologies if any of them seem like I'm stating the bleeding obvious.

• Firstly, buy in season. You'll always hear chefs on the telly talking about seasonal produce and they do so with good reason. Fruit and vegetables in season will always taste better and be in abundance, meaning greater availability and lower prices. The trouble is that with supermarket supply chains we have access to a huge range of produce throughout the year, which can often skew our perception of seasonality. I'm not suggesting that you exclusively buy locally grown produce as it's just not practical, but simply that an awareness of when things are in their prime is handy if you want to get the best flavour. This isn't so much of an issue when buying meat — a steak will taste just as good whenever you buy it — but if your dish relies on something like asparagus, it'll taste infinitely better during

that short, frenzied season at the start of spring (when I eat the stuff like it's going out of fashion).

• Try to look beyond the supermarkets. While they're great for consistency and convenience, they'll be limited by what's in their range and what's viable on a large scale. If you have a local farmers' market, then pop along and see what looks good; you'll usually find the stallholders to be well-informed and full of advice about how to cook their produce. A little tip though; visit markets at the start of the day when you'll have the pick of the best produce; a basket of wild mushrooms or bunches of rainbow chard will get snapped up by the early birds. Then go for a coffee or a bite to eat and go back to the market as it's closing to pick up any bargains to be had.

• When you're choosing vegetables, don't just look, use your hands too. Get used to picking up fruit and vegetables to get a feel for them. Most vegetables should feel firm and heavy when they're at their peak as they're full of water. If a cauliflower or cabbage feels a little lighter or more limp, it's because it's old and losing water. Not necessarily a bad thing; older vegetables are fine in soups and stews where liquid is being added anyway, or when roasted (where you're aiming to reduce the moisture and caramelise the natural sugars). Just try not to be overzealous with prodding and poking; I'm sure I'm not the only one who's felt obliged to buy an avocado after squeezing a little too hard and putting a thumb through it!

I've tried to keep this book vegetarian, although some recipes do call for cheeses such as feta or Parmesan which are commonly made using rennet, an enzyme that comes from cattle. There are vegetarian versions of these cheeses available, but if you follow a strictly meat-free diet, then the chances are you'll be better informed than I am on where to source them and which brands are best. One of the biggest challenges was creating South-east Asian recipes without fish sauce as it lends such a distinctive flavour, so after much trial and error (and having to submit my poor wife to numerous rounds of taste testing) I came up with No-fish Sauce (page 205); all the funk but no fish. If you're not strictly veggie then you can just use regular fish sauce in the same quantities. Likewise with stock; all of the recipes are based around a flavourful vegetable stock, but if you happen to have chicken stock in the freezer or a stock cube in the cupboard then by all means use it.

These recipes aren't prescriptive and should be approached with an open mind and the knowledge that there's no harm in tweaking them to your own taste or simply to suit what you have in the fridge. One of the most satisfying things is to hear that people have cooked from my books but with the odd change or addition; it shows me that my recipes are being used as a starting point for people getting excited about cooking and being creative in the kitchen. If recipes are approached as a set of strict rules that must be obeyed to the letter, then cooking ceases to be fun, and if

it's not fun, then what's the point? The only exception tends to be baking, where quantities, times and temperatures are a little more important, but otherwise there's no harm in using alternatives as you see fit. For example, butternut squash and pumpkin are generally interchangeable, regular broccoli works just as well as Tenderstem, and if you can't find baby vegetables just buy the grown-up size and get busy with your knife. And don't go out of your way to find every ingredient on the list; if you're missing the odd spice or fresh herb, the dish won't suffer too greatly as a result. However you approach the recipes in this book, whether you're a vegetarian or not, I hope that you enjoy cooking them as much as I enjoyed creating them.

MORNING

Huevos Divorciados

SERVES 4

I love to start the day with bit of a chilli kick; it wakes up the taste buds and helps to clear the cobwebs from the night before. The name of this dish literally means 'divorced eggs' and refers to the two vibrant sauces which are always served separately. The beauty of this recipe is that you can make both sauces and the beans the night before, so it's just a case of frying some eggs and mixing a bloody Mary the following day.

sea salt

FOR THE RED SAUCE:
3 large, ripe tomatoes, quartered
1 red chilli
1 garlic clove, unpeeled

FOR THE GREEN SAUCE:
½ white onion, peeled and cut into wedges
1 green chilli
1 garlic clove, peeled and crushed
5 tomatillos, fresh or canned
1 small bunch of coriander, roughly chopped

FOR THE BEANS:
400g can black beans, drained and rinsed
1 teaspoon ground cumin
1 teaspoon hot smoked paprika
juice of ½ lime

TO SERVE:
olive oil, for frying
8 medium eggs
8 small corn tortillas, toasted
100g feta, crumbled

Preheat the oven to 220°C/gas mark 7. Line a baking tray with greaseproof paper and arrange the ingredients for both sauces, except the tomatillos if using the canned variety and the coriander for the green sauce, in an even layer. Roast for 15 minutes until everything is blistered and beginning to soften.

Remove from the oven and leave until cool enough to handle, then peel the garlic and remove the stems from the chillies. Transfer the roasted ingredients for the red sauce to a food processor and blend until smooth, then pour into a bowl. Rinse out the food processor, add the roasted ingredients for the green sauce, tomatillos and coriander and blend until smooth, then pour into a separate bowl. Season both sauces to taste with salt.

Combine the beans, cumin and paprika in a saucepan with a splash of water. Bring to a simmer and cook gently for 5 minutes. Roughly mash the beans with a fork, stir through the lime juice and season to taste with salt.

When you're ready to serve, heat two frying pans and add a generous splash of olive oil to each. Fry the eggs until the whites are set, then baste with the oil to set the tops; I like my yolks runny and the edges of the whites golden and crisp.

Spread the toasted tortillas with the bean mixture and top each with a fried egg so that everyone has two each. Top one egg on each plate with red sauce and the other with green sauce. Scatter over the feta and serve.

NOTE: It's not easy to get hold of fresh tomatillos, but plenty of specialist shops and online retailers sell the canned variety, which work really well in this recipe. Alternatively, you can use underripe, green tomatoes, which you will need to roast as with fresh tomatillos, but you may need to add a pinch of sugar.

Duck Eggs with Spinach and Chermoula

SERVES 4

This recipe is somewhere between eggs Florentine and Shakshuka — a North African dish of eggs cooked in a rich, spicy tomato sauce — but it's a little lighter and far quicker to prepare. If you want to get ahead, you can prepare the base of the chermoula the night before; just leave out the coriander and stir it through just before serving.

splash of olive oil
600g large-leaf spinach, washed and stalks removed
pinch of sea salt
4 duck eggs
3 tablespoons natural yogurt

FOR THE CHERMOULA:
1 preserved lemon
1 small garlic clove, peeled and crushed
1 small bunch of coriander
juice of ½ lemon
1 teaspoon cumin seeds, toasted
½ teaspoon hot smoked paprika
½ teaspoon dried chilli flakes
extra virgin olive oil
sea salt, if needed

buttered sourdough toast, to serve

First make the chermoula. Quarter the preserved lemon and use the side of a teaspoon to scrape out the flesh and discard; you're only after the skin as the flesh is too bitter. Finely chop the skin, then put in a food processor with the remaining ingredients, except the extra virgin olive oil and salt. Start blending and then, with the motor running, gradually add enough oil to make a smooth sauce. Season if it needs it — preserved lemon can be quite salty, so do taste the chermoula before adding any salt.

Heat the olive oil in a large frying pan, add the spinach with the salt and fry over a high heat for 2–3 minutes until wilted. Make four wells in the spinach and crack an egg into each, then cover the pan and cook gently for 3–4 minutes until the whites are just set but the yolks are still runny.

Drizzle over the yogurt and chermoula, put the whole pan in the middle of the table with a stack of buttered sourdough toast and let everyone dive in.

Sweet Potato Cinnamon Rolls

MAKES 12

These rolls are the ultimate weekend breakfast treat; light, fluffy and packed with sweet cinnamon butter. The addition of sweet potato makes them incredibly soft and moist, perfect for tearing into and eating with a good cup of coffee. If you make the dough the night before, it's just a matter of rolling and baking the rolls in the morning. Your kitchen will smell incredible and you'll suddenly be very popular.

500g strong white
  bread flour
1 teaspoon fine sea salt
2 x 7g sachets fast-
  action dried yeast
150ml warm whole milk
150g butter, melted, plus
  extra for greasing
150g mashed
  sweet potato
75g golden caster sugar
3 medium egg yolks,
  plus 1 medium egg
  yolk, beaten, for sealing

FOR THE FILLING:
100g butter, softened
50g golden caster sugar
50g light brown
  soft sugar
2 tablespoons
  ground cinnamon

FOR THE GLAZE:
150g icing sugar, sifted
75g cream cheese
1 tablespoon whole milk

Put the flour and salt in the bowl of a stand mixer fitted with a dough hook, then add the yeast, keeping it away from the salt. In a large jug, whisk together the milk, butter, mashed sweet potato, sugar and egg yolks. Pour the mixture into the flour, then knead on a medium speed for 5 minutes. Increase the speed slightly and knead for a further 2 minutes.

Tip the dough into a lightly greased bowl, cover and leave in a warm place for 1 hour until doubled in size. Transfer the bowl to the fridge for a further hour, which will allow the butter to firm up, making the dough easier to roll later.

Meanwhile, put all the filling ingredients in a bowl and beat together until smooth, then set aside.

Roll the dough out on a work surface into a thin rectangle, 35 x 70cm. Starting at the edge nearest to you, spread the filling over half the dough in an even layer, leaving a 2cm gap along the edge furthest from you. Fold the uncovered half of the dough back towards you to completely enclose the filling, then roll over a couple of times with the rolling pin to seal. Roll up the dough tightly, pulling the roll back towards you as you go to create a tight seal. Brush the furthest edge with the beaten egg yolk, then pinch along the whole length to seal it in place – ensure that the edge is well sealed, otherwise the rolls may unravel during baking.

CONTINUED OVERLEAF

Sweet Potato Cinnamon Rolls continued

The trick to keeping the cinnamon rolls a nice round shape is not to cut them with a knife because, no matter how sharp it may be, as you press down on the dough log, it will flatten slightly and the rolls will end up an oval shape. Instead, loop a length of cotton under the dough log, cross it over the top and pull tightly to slice it into perfect rounds. Repeat down the length of the log to create 12 equal slices.

Divide the slices between two deep 8-hole muffin tins, cover with clingfilm and transfer to the fridge for 30 minutes. Meanwhile, preheat the oven to 180°C/gas mark 4.

Remove the clingfilm and bake the rolls for 15 minutes, then cover with a sheet of foil and bake for a further 7–8 minutes. While the rolls are baking, beat together the icing sugar, cream cheese and milk for the glaze.

Remove the rolls from the oven then brush the cream cheese glaze over the tops. The heat of the rolls will melt the glaze and it'll find its way into all the nooks and crannies. Leave to cool for 10 minutes, then serve warm with coffee.

Sweetcorn French Toast with Blueberries

SERVES 4

Proper French Toast should be made from doorstep-thick slabs of good-quality white bread, nothing fancy like brioche as it's too soft and the end result will be soggy. The only exception to the rule is challah, a rich, slightly sweet Jewish bread that's slightly harder to track down but makes beautiful French Toast. The sweetcorn purée in this recipe isn't just for colour and flavour, it's full of starch which thickens as the batter is cooked, creating a custardy centre and crisp, golden edges.

4 thick slices of day-old
  white bread or challah
200g can sweetcorn,
  drained
300ml whole milk
4 large eggs
2 tablespoons maple
  syrup, plus extra
  to serve
2 tablespoons Brown
  Butter (page 205)
pinch of fine sea salt
vegetable oil, for frying
butter, for frying

TO SERVE:
1 tablespoon icing sugar
1 teaspoon
  ground cinnamon
300g blueberries

Preheat the oven to 75°C/gas mark ¼. Arrange the slices of bread on a wire rack, then bake in the oven for 20 minutes to dry them out.

Meanwhile, make the batter. Put the sweetcorn and milk into a liquidiser and blend until smooth. Strain through a fine sieve into a large bowl, pressing down on the purée with the back of a spoon to extract as much liquid as possible. Whisk in the eggs, maple syrup, Brown Butter and salt until smooth.

Lay the bread slices in a shallow roasting tin and pour over the batter, turning each piece to coat. Leave to soak for 5 minutes, turning the slices occasionally; they should soak up almost all the liquid.

Heat a little oil and butter in a large, non-stick frying pan and fry the soaked bread slices for 2 minutes on each side – you may need to do this in batches or use two frying pans at the same time.

Mix together the icing sugar and cinnamon, then dust over the hot French toast. Serve with the blueberries and plenty of maple syrup.

NOTE: You can dry the bread out and make the batter the night before to make things easier in the morning. Just don't add the Brown Butter to the batter until you're ready to cook, otherwise it will solidify.

IMAGE SHOWN OVERLEAF

Mushroom and Spinach Hash with Mustard Sauce

SERVES 4

I love a breakfast hash; essentially the end result of a spot of fridge-raiding topped off with a runny egg. I often have a handful of leftover potatoes so they tend to be the starting point, then it's just a case of adding whatever you have to hand. This version poshes it up a little with the addition of wild mushrooms and a quick mustard sauce.

fine sea salt
400g Charlotte
    potatoes, cut into
    2cm pieces
olive oil
25g butter
2 onions, peeled and
    finely sliced
1 garlic clove, peeled
    and crushed
400g mixed wild
    mushrooms, sliced
400g baby leaf spinach,
    washed
4 medium eggs

FOR THE MUSTARD SAUCE:
100ml double cream
1 tablespoon
    wholegrain mustard
1 teaspoon
    Dijon mustard

slices of toast, to serve

Bring a pan of salted water to the boil, add the potatoes and cook for 8 minutes or until just tender. Drain and set aside to steam.

Meanwhile, heat a splash of olive oil and the butter in a large, cast-iron pan, add the onions and garlic and fry gently for 10 minutes until softened and caramelised. Increase the heat, add the mushrooms and cook for a further 5 minutes.

While the onions and mushrooms are frying, blanch the spinach in a pan of boiling water for 30 seconds, then drain and squeeze out as much excess liquid as possible.

Remove the onions and mushrooms from the pan and set aside. Set the pan over a high heat, add a little more olive oil followed by the potatoes and fry for 5 minutes until golden and crisp. Return the onions and mushrooms to the pan. Roughly chop the spinach, add to the pan and toss to combine.

While the potatoes are frying, poach the eggs in a separate pan of gently simmering water for 3–4 minutes, then drain. At the same time, combine the ingredients for the mustard sauce in a small saucepan and bring to the boil, then reduce the heat and simmer for 2–3 minutes until thickened. Remove the pan from the heat.

Serve the hash and poached eggs with the mustard sauce and slices of toast for dipping.

Carrot Cake Granola

SERVES 6–8

This recipe came about after a recent trip to New York, where I had an amazing carrot cake muffin for breakfast one morning. It wasn't as sweet as a normal cake, but was packed with the flavour of carrots, cinnamon, orange and raisins. I'm far too lazy to make a fresh batch of muffins every morning so a granola version was the obvious choice; you can make a big batch of it, store it in an airtight container and it'll last for a good few weeks.

150g rolled oats
100g mixed seeds, such as sunflower, pumpkin, sesame and linseeds
100g pecans
2 teaspoons ground cinnamon, plus extra to serve
pinch of sea salt
4 tablespoons maple syrup
2 tablespoons vegetable oil
1 large carrot, peeled and grated
1 apple, cored and grated
finely grated zest of 1 unwaxed orange
150g raisins

TO SERVE:
200ml natural yogurt
100g cream cheese
finely grated zest of 1 unwaxed lemon

Preheat the oven to 160°C/gas mark 3. Put all the main ingredients, except the raisins, into a large bowl. Scrunch everything together with your hands to break up the nuts and mix together, then tip onto a large baking tray and spread out evenly (or divide between two smaller trays).

Bake for 30 minutes until golden and crisp, stirring halfway through cooking.

Remove from the oven, stir through the raisins and then bake for a further 10 minutes. Remove from the oven and leave to cool completely.

To serve, stir the yogurt, cream cheese and lemon zest together, then spoon over the granola and top with an extra pinch of cinnamon.

Beetroot Bircher Muesli

SERVES 6

Thanks to my job and the fact that we have a very energetic toddler, I'm always up really early and things get busy pretty quickly. As a result, it's often tricky to find the time to make a decent, healthy breakfast so a bit of forward-planning is crucial. Bircher muesli is the perfect solution as it only takes a few minutes to throw together the night before, and the next morning you have something vibrant and delicious to really enjoy for breakfast.

150g porridge oats
1 medium beetroot,
  peeled and grated
75g dried cranberries
300ml fresh apple juice
2 apples, such as
  Cox or Braeburn,
  cored and grated
4 tablespoons
  natural yogurt, plus
  extra to serve
150g blackberries
ground cinnamon,
  to serve

Combine the oats, grated beetroot and dried cranberries in a bowl. Stir in the apple juice, then cover and chill in the fridge overnight.

The next morning, remove the bowl from the fridge and stir through the grated apple and yogurt.

Divide between serving bowls and top with an extra spoonful of the yogurt, a handful of blackberries and a pinch of cinnamon.

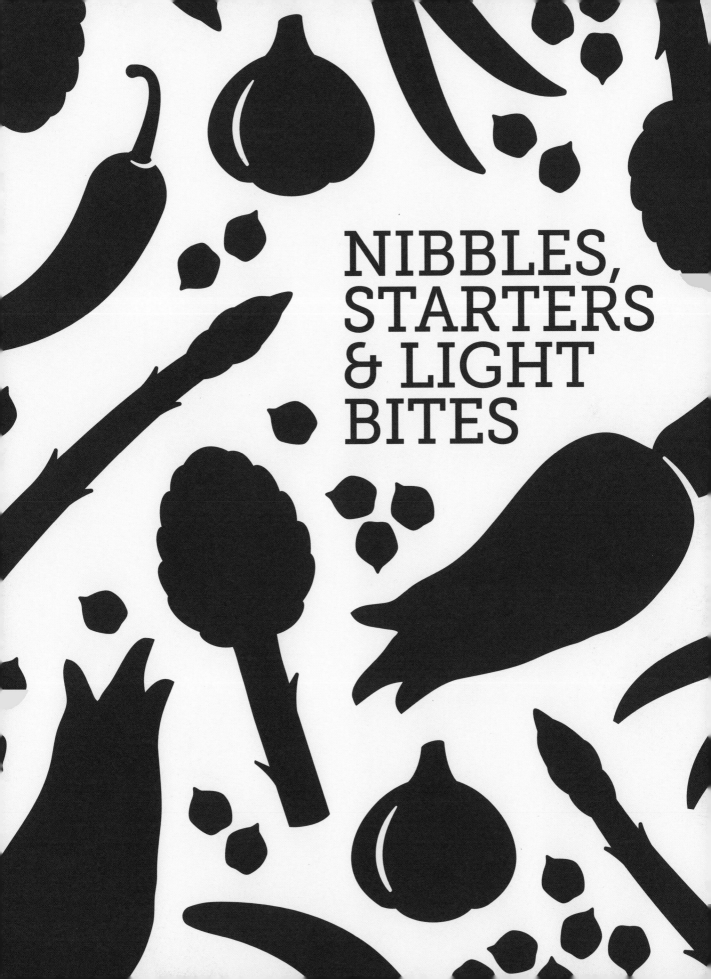

NIBBLES, STARTERS & LIGHT BITES

Asparagus with Fresh Goat's Curd and Crispy Capers

**SERVES 4
AS A SIDE**

There's something incredibly satisfying about making food from scratch, be it ice cream, bread, pasta or, in this case, cheese. Curd cheese is very much entry-level, with no rennet involved and very little chance of anything going disastrously wrong. The reward is beautifully soft, lemony goat's curd with a little tang to go with the grassy asparagus. Of course, this dish is equally tasty with a shop-bought curd; just beat in a squeeze of lemon juice to give it a little zing.

olive oil
2 tablespoons small
   capers, drained and
   patted dry with kitchen
   paper
fine sea salt
600g asparagus,
   trimmed
Lemon Oil
   (page 203)
finely grated zest of
   1 unwaxed lemon

FOR THE GOAT'S CURD:
1 litre goat's milk
40ml lemon juice
   (you'll need
   1–2 lemons)
1 teaspoon fine sea salt

For the goat's curd, pour the milk into a saucepan and heat gently until it begins to steam; if you have a thermometer, it should reach 80°C. Remove the pan from the heat, sprinkle the lemon juice over the milk and then leave to cool completely – don't stir. As the milk cools, it will separate into curds and whey.

Line a colander with lightly dampened muslin cloth, then slowly and carefully ladle in the curds and whey. Leave to drain for 10 minutes, then gather up the edges of the cloth and tie together to make a bag. Hang the bag over a bowl to catch the liquid that drains out and transfer to the fridge. The curd will be ready to use after an hour, but if you prefer a firmer, more crumbly cheese, then leave the curd to hang overnight.

Either way, once you're ready to use the curd, spread it out on a plate and gently work the salt in with your fingertips, then return the curd to the fridge.

Heat a glug of olive oil in a frying pan, add the capers and fry gently for 5 minutes until crisp, stirring occasionally. You'll know when they're ready by the sound they make; as you stir them in the pan, they'll start to rustle. Remove with a slotted spoon and drain on kitchen paper.

Bring a large pan of salted water to the boil, add the asparagus and blanch for 2–3 minutes, depending on the thickness of the spears. Drain thoroughly, then toss with a little Lemon Oil.

Spread the goat's curd on a serving plate, arrange the asparagus on top and scatter over the capers. Finish with the lemon zest and a little extra Lemon Oil.

Caponata

SERVES 4–6

One of my favourite food destinations has to be Sicily; the fresh produce is incredible, the dishes are always simple and delicious and the Sicilians are fiercely proud of the food they produce and serve. In my eyes Caponata is the dish of Sicily; it's a simple collection of ingredients made better than the sum of their parts through slow, careful cooking. And like so many Sicilian dishes, no two Caponatas are ever the same. There are so many variations that it's impossible to say what constitutes a truly authentic version, but the common denominator has to be the sweet and sour flavour. A good caponata should have plenty of vinegar and a level of sweetness from slow cooking whilst still retaining the texture of the individual vegetables.

olive oil
2 large aubergines,
    cut into 2cm chunks
sea salt
2 medium courgettes,
    cut into 2cm chunks
1 onion, peeled and
    chopped
1 celery stick, chopped
1 tablespoon
    caster sugar
150ml red wine vinegar
2 tablespoons
    tomato purée
3 plum tomatoes,
    peeled and diced
50g pitted black olives,
    torn
200ml passata
1 small bunch of basil,
    leaves picked and torn
freshly ground black
    pepper
grilled sourdough,
    to serve (optional)

Heat a few spoonfuls of olive oil in a large frying pan, add half the aubergines and fry over a medium–high heat for 7–8 minutes until deep brown and caramelised, adding a pinch of salt towards the end of cooking. Transfer to a large plate or bowl. Repeat with the remaining aubergines and the courgettes, each time seasoning towards the end (adding salt too early will draw the moisture from the vegetables so that they'll stew rather than caramelise).

Add more oil to the pan and fry the onion and celery for 8–10 minutes until soft and starting to turn golden. Sprinkle in the sugar and pour in the vinegar, then leave to bubble for a couple of minutes. Stir in the tomato purée and cook for a further minute or so, then add the tomatoes and simmer for about 10 minutes until they start to break down.

Return the fried vegetables to the pan along with the olives and passata. Bring to a simmer, then cover the pan, reduce the heat and cook gently for 30 minutes.

Remove the pan from the heat and leave to cool to room temperature. Stir through the torn basil and season to taste with salt and black pepper. The caponata is ready to eat straight away, but really benefits from a night in the fridge to allow the flavours to develop. Serve on its own as part of an antipasti, on top of some slices of grilled sourdough or as part of the Gnocchi with Caponata and Burrata Cream (page 89).

Togarashi Padrón Peppers

**SERVES 4
AS A SNACK**

Padrón peppers are my go-to snack to serve with a chilled sherry or a cold beer. Some craft beers have pretty bold flavours so I wanted to come up with a simple snack with a bit of a kick to serve with them. Togarashi seasoning made perfect sense; it's got a bit of heat and a lovely nuttiness from the sesame seeds.

15g butter, softened
2 teaspoons
  shichimi togarashi
400g Padrón peppers
splash of olive oil
pinch of sea salt flakes

Beat together the butter and shichimi togarashi in a small bowl and set aside.

Heat a large, dry frying pan over a high heat until smoking. Add the peppers and fry, turning regularly, for 3–4 minutes until they start to blister. Add the olive oil and fry for a further minute, then tip into a large bowl.

Add the butter to the peppers, toss to coat, then tip onto a warmed serving plate. Scatter over the sea salt and serve.

Green Gazpacho

SERVES 4

This makes a great starter, particularly before a barbecue, as it wakes up your palate without being too filling. I pile up the ingredients in a liquidiser jug and pop it into the fridge along with serving glasses or small bowls. Then it just needs to be blended and poured, leaving plenty of time to light the barbecue and crack open a bottle.

2 green peppers
1 day-old slice of white
  bread, crusts removed
1 cucumber, peeled,
  deseeded and
  roughly chopped
4 spring onions,
  roughly chopped
1 green chilli, deseeded
  and roughly chopped
75g baby leaf spinach,
  washed
1 small bunch of basil,
  leaves picked

2 tablespoons
  cider vinegar
2 tablespoons
  extra virgin olive oil,
  plus extra to serve
pinch of caster sugar
sea salt and freshly
  ground black pepper

FOR THE PICKLED APPLE:
2 tablespoons
  cider vinegar
½ teaspoon caster sugar
1 Granny Smith apple

a few sprigs of mint,
  leaves picked, to serve

Preheat the oven to 220°C/gas mark 7. Line a baking tray with greaseproof paper, lay the peppers on it and roast for 20 minutes, turning halfway through. Transfer to a bowl, cover with clingfilm and leave to cool.

Meanwhile, make the pickled apple. Whisk together the vinegar, sugar and a pinch of salt in a small bowl. Peel and core the apple, then slice into thin matchsticks. Toss in the vinegar, then cover with clingfilm and chill.

Peel the peppers and discard the seeds and stalks. Put the flesh in a liquidiser with the remaining ingredients, add a splash of water and blend until smooth. Season to taste.

Divide the gazpacho between serving bowls and drizzle with a little oil. Drain the pickled apple, divide between the bowls and finish with a few mint leaves.

IMAGES SHOWN OVERLEAF

Mushroom Croquetas with Tarragon Aioli

MAKES 18

These crispy little balls of tapas delight are traditionally made with finely chopped ham and fried leeks, but you can flavour them with all sorts of ingredients. The key is getting the béchamel sauce right; it needs to be cooked until it cleanly pulls away from the sides of the pan. This way it'll be thick enough to roll into balls when it's cool and will then turn almost liquid when fried.

2 tablespoons olive oil, plus extra for oiling
250g chestnut mushrooms, stalks removed, finely chopped
25g butter
50g plain flour
20g porcini powder, plus extra to serve
400ml whole milk
sea salt and freshly ground black pepper

FOR THE TARRAGON AIOLI:
1 medium egg yolk
1 garlic clove, peeled and crushed
good pinch of fine sea salt
100ml vegetable oil
2 tablespoons extra virgin olive oil
1 teaspoon tarragon vinegar or white wine vinegar
1 bunch of tarragon, leaves picked and finely chopped

FOR FRYING THE CROQUETAS:
vegetable oil, for deep-frying
100g plain flour
3 medium eggs, beaten
100g fine white breadcrumbs

Heat the olive oil in a large saucepan over a high heat, add the mushrooms and fry for 10 minutes until all the moisture has been cooked off and they start to caramelise. Add the butter and flour and cook, stirring, for 5 minutes until the mixture smells nutty. Stir in the porcini powder, then gradually beat in the milk. Once all the milk has been incorporated, simmer for 5 minutes, stirring regularly, until thickened and starting to pull away from the sides of the pan. Pour the mixture into a small, lightly oiled baking tray, then press a sheet of clingfilm onto the surface to stop a skin from forming. Chill in the fridge for 1 hour until firm.

Meanwhile, make the aioli. Put the egg yolk and garlic in a bowl, add the salt and whisk together until smooth. Combine the oils in a jug and, whisking constantly, begin to pour the oil into the bowl in a very thin, steady stream. It's crucial that you really take your time at this stage; over-zealous oil pouring will result in splitting. Continue steadily adding the oil, still whisking constantly, until it's all incorporated. Stir in the vinegar and tarragon.

To fry the croquetas, heat the vegetable oil in a large pan to 160°C. Lightly flour your hands, then roll the mushroom mixture into 18 equal balls; each should be roughly the size of a walnut. Put the flour, beaten eggs and breadcrumbs in three shallow bowls. Roll each ball in flour, then in the beaten egg and finally in the breadcrumbs. Repeat the process with each croqueta to give them a double coating. Deep-fry, in batches, for 2–3 minutes until golden and crisp, then remove from the oil and drain on kitchen paper. Season with a little salt and porcini powder and serve with the tarragon aioli.

Roast Carrot Hummus

SERVES 4–6

Whilst it's possible to find some pretty good hummus in the shops, you really can't beat homemade. I like the sweetness of the roasted carrots as they work perfectly with a bit of spice, but feel free to use this recipe as a bit of a template for different roast vegetable combinations. I've also made this with a handful of grilled veggies I found lurking in the fridge after a barbecue. Try to find the fat, creamy jarred chickpeas as they tend to have a bit more flavour than the canned ones.

4 carrots, scrubbed
  and halved lengthways
4 garlic cloves, unpeeled
3 tablespoons olive oil
570g jar chickpeas,
  drained and rinsed
1 teaspoon
  smoked paprika
1 teaspoon
  ground cumin
juice of 1 lemon
2 tablespoons tahini
2 tablespoons
  extra virgin olive oil,
  plus extra to serve
sea salt
½ teaspoon
  ground sumac

Preheat the oven to 160°C/gas mark 3. Line a baking tray with greaseproof paper. Arrange the carrots and garlic on the lined tray in a single layer, pour over the olive oil and roast for 1 hour.

Scatter the chickpeas over the carrots and garlic and sprinkle over the smoked paprika and cumin, then roast for a further 10 minutes.

Remove from the oven and leave until the garlic cloves are cool enough to handle, then squeeze the roasted garlic flesh from its skins. Tip into a food processor with the remaining contents of the tray, add the lemon juice, tahini and extra virgin olive oil and blend until smooth, seasoning to taste with salt as you go.

Spoon the hummus into a serving bowl, sprinkle with the sumac and drizzle with more extra virgin olive oil.

Panelle

MAKES 36–40

I discovered these simple little chickpea fritters on a trip to Sicily. Wild fennel grows in abundance on the island and is often used in the batter so I've used fennel seeds for a similar flavour. Make sure the cooked batter is chilled before cutting so that the fritters hold their shape as they're fried. And be generous with the seasoning.

1 tablespoon fennel
   seeds, ground in
   a pestle and mortar
   or spice grinder
300g chickpea flour
900ml water
fine sea salt
olive oil, for oiling
   and frying

Put the ground fennel seeds, chickpea flour, water and a generous pinch of salt into a saucepan and whisk together until smooth.

Set the pan over a medium heat and bring to a simmer. Cook, whisking constantly, for 8–10 minutes until thickened. Pour into an oiled baking tray and smooth with the back of a wet spoon. Leave to cool completely.

Turn the dough out onto a lightly oiled chopping board and cut into rectangles or small triangles. Heat 1cm oil in a wide, shallow pan over a medium heat and fry, in batches, for a couple of minutes on each side until crisp. Drain on kitchen paper, season with salt and serve.

Crispy Chickpeas

**SERVES 4
AS A SNACK**

These crunchy, zesty chickpeas make a great snack to serve alongside drinks. I always end up making a double batch as they quickly disappear. If you do this, spread them out over a couple of baking trays so that they cook in a crisp, even layer.

2 teaspoons
   fine sea salt
2 teaspoons
   caster sugar
4 teaspoons
   boiling water
2 teaspoons
   chilli powder
2 teaspoons
   garlic powder
2 tablespoons
   rapeseed or olive oil
2 x 570g jars chickpeas,
   drained and rinsed
2 unwaxed limes

Preheat the oven to 180°C/gas mark 4. Line a baking tray with greaseproof paper.

Combine the salt and sugar in a large bowl, pour over the water and whisk until both have dissolved. Whisk in the chilli, garlic powder and oil until emulsified, then set aside.

Spread the chickpeas out in a single layer on a clean tea towel, cover with a second tea towel and rub gently in a circular motion to remove the skins – the odd few may need peeling by hand. Tip the chickpeas into the bowl with the oil mixture and toss to coat.

Transfer the chickpeas to the lined baking tray, reserving the bowl for later. Bake for 40 minutes, shaking the tray a couple of times during cooking. Remove from the oven, tip the chickpeas into the reserved bowl and finely grate over the lime zest. Toss the chickpeas to coat, then tip them back onto the baking tray and leave to cool completely.

Spicy Aubergine with Crispy Rice

MAKES 24

I'm fortunate enough to go on some pretty amazing trips to New York with my brother, and as soon as we've booked our flights, attention turns to the most important task – deciding where to eat and drink. New York is my favourite city in the world when it comes to restaurants and has played host to some incredible meals (and fairly savage hangovers). One restaurant we migrate to when our heads are sore from the previous night is Catch, a fish and seafood restaurant in the Meatpacking District. They make these tiny squares of crispy rice topped with minced raw tuna and a fierce kick of chilli. A plateful of these is enough to clear the cobwebs, so this is my version, where soft, sweet aubergine replaces the tuna.

FOR THE RICE:
180g sushi rice, rinsed
250ml water
½ teaspoon fine sea salt
½ teaspoon caster sugar
2 tablespoons
  rice vinegar
vegetable oil, for oiling
  and deep-frying

FOR THE AUBERGINE:
vegetable oil
1 medium aubergine,
  very finely diced
3 spring onions,
  white parts only,
  finely chopped
2 tablespoons sriracha
  hot sauce
1 tablespoon Kewpie
  (Japanese)
  mayonnaise or
  regular mayonnaise
1 teaspoon rice vinegar

TO FINISH:
shichimi togarashi
3 spring onions, green
  parts only, finely
  chopped

For the rice, put the rinsed rice and water in a saucepan and bring to the boil, then immediately reduce the heat to its lowest setting. Cover the pan and cook for 10 minutes. Remove the pan from the heat and set aside for 10 minutes with the lid on.

Meanwhile, stir the salt and sugar together with the vinegar in a bowl until dissolved.

Once the standing time for the rice is up, pour over the dressing and stir with a fork to coat the grains evenly, then leave to cool.

Line a 20 x 10cm loaf tin with clingfilm, press the rice into the base of the tin and cover with another piece of clingfilm. Chill for 30 minutes. Turn out and cut into 24 cubes; a lightly oiled knife makes this much easier.

For the aubergine, heat a little vegetable oil in a large frying pan, add half the aubergine and fry over a high heat for 5 minutes until softened and caramelised. Tip onto a plate lined with kitchen paper and squeeze to remove as much excess oil as possible. Repeat with the remaining aubergine. Return all the aubergine to the pan, add the spring onions and fry for a further 2 minutes. Remove the pan from the heat, then stir in the sriracha, mayonnaise and vinegar. Leave to cool to room temperature.

Heat the vegetable oil for deep-frying in a large saucepan to 180°C. Fry the rice cubes, in batches, for 1–2 minutes until the edges are just starting to turn golden. Remove from the oil and drain on kitchen paper.

To serve, top the rice cubes with the aubergine mixture, season with shichimi togarashi and finish each with a little of the spring onion greens.

Onion Rava Dosa

SERVES 4

I first tried this at a roadside stall in Delhi where I was watching the cooks turn out enormous, paper-thin dosa stuffed with potato masala. But it was the rava dosa, rava meaning semolina in Hindi, that really caught my attention. As soon as the batter hit the griddle it spread out into a lacy disc flecked with onions and chilli. The texture is perfect — golden and crisp at the edges, the centre softened by the heat of the masala.

FOR THE COCONUT CHUTNEY:
100g fresh coconut, grated
20g peeled fresh ginger, grated
1 medium green chilli, roughly chopped
juice of ½ lemon
pinch of sea salt
1 tablespoon coconut oil or vegetable oil
1 teaspoon black mustard seeds
15 fresh curry leaves

FOR THE POTATO MASALA:
vegetable oil
2 teaspoons black mustard seeds
1 teaspoon cumin seeds
2 dried red chillies, crumbled
2 onions, peeled and finely chopped
3 garlic cloves, peeled and crushed
12 fresh curry leaves
4 medium floury potatoes, peeled and cubed
1 teaspoon ground turmeric
1 teaspoon fine sea salt
600ml water
1 small bunch of coriander, finely chopped

FOR THE DOSA:
100g coarse semolina
100g rice flour
50g plain flour
1 sweet white onion, peeled and finely chopped
2 green chillies, finely chopped
12 fresh curry leaves, chopped
1 teaspoon fine sea salt
550–600ml water
vegetable oil, for frying
1 teaspoon black mustard seeds
1 teaspoon cumin seeds
½ teaspoon crushed black peppercorns

First make the chutney. Put the coconut, ginger, chilli and lemon juice in a liquidiser and add a splash of water and the salt. Blend until smooth, then pour into a small bowl. Heat the oil in a small frying pan over a medium heat, add the mustard seeds and curry leaves and fry for a couple of minutes until the mustard seeds start to pop and the leaves turn crisp. Pour into the bowl with the puréed coconut mixture and stir together. Set aside.

For the potato masala, heat a splash of vegetable oil in a saucepan over a medium heat, add the mustard seeds, cumin seeds and chillies and fry for a couple of minutes until the mustard seeds start to pop. Add the onions and fry gently for 10 minutes until softened. Add the garlic and curry leaves and fry for a further couple of minutes, then stir in the potatoes, turmeric and salt and pour in the water. Cook for 15 minutes until the potatoes have softened and are starting to break up. Remove the pan from the heat, then roughly crush a few of the potatoes and stir through the coriander.

To make the dosa, whisk the semolina, flours, onion, chillies, curry leaves and salt with the water, adding enough until you have a very thin batter; it needs to be a very thin consistency to create crisp, lacy pancakes. Heat a little vegetable oil in a small frying pan over a medium heat, add the mustard seeds, cumin seeds and crushed peppercorns and fry for a minute until fragrant. Pour into the batter and whisk to combine.

Heat a little vegetable oil in a large, non-stick frying pan over a medium heat, add a ladleful of the batter — it should spread out to a very thin layer and quickly turn lacy. If the batter is too thick, the pancake won't cook evenly and will be difficult to flip. Fry the pancake for 1 minute on each side, then transfer to a warmed serving plate. Cook the remaining batter in the same way.

To serve, spoon the potato masala into the centre of the pancakes, then fold the edges in to make an open square parcel. Serve with the coconut chutney.

**SERVES 4
AS A STARTER
OR SERVES 2
AS A MAIN**

King Oyster Larb

I said at the start of this book that I wasn't going to include any 'meat replacement' recipes, and I still stand firm on that. However, if you're trying to cut back on meat or want to please a mixed crowd of veggies and non-veggies then the dense, meaty King Oyster mushroom is a great place to start. This is my version of a dish that originates in Laos, but I've always eaten it in Thailand or in Thai restaurants back home. It should have that perfect balance of hot, sweet, salty and sour, finished with the crunch of toasted rice. If you're preparing this in a hot kitchen, keep the lettuce leaves in a bowl of iced water until you're ready to serve so that they stay crisp.

1 tablespoon uncooked
  Thai sticky rice
3 tablespoons No-fish
  Sauce (page 205)
juice of 2 limes
1 tablespoon palm sugar
2 tablespoons
  groundnut oil
3 garlic cloves, peeled
  and chopped
2 red bird's-eye chillies,
  deseeded and
  finely sliced
4 Kaffir lime leaves,
  stems removed,
  finely chopped
a thumb-sized piece
  of galangal, peeled
  and finely chopped
500g King Oyster
  mushrooms, very
  finely chopped
6 Thai shallots, peeled
  and finely sliced
1 small bunch of
  coriander, leaves picked
  and roughly chopped
1 small bunch of Thai
  basil, leaves picked and
  roughly chopped
1 small bunch of mint,
  leaves picked and
  roughly chopped
3 Baby Gem lettuces,
  leaves separated
cooked Thai sticky rice,
  to serve

Heat a dry wok over a medium heat, add the rice and toast for 2–3 minutes until lightly browned. Using a pestle and mortar, grind the toasted rice to a fine powder. Set aside.

Stir together the No-fish Sauce, lime juice and palm sugar in a small bowl until the sugar has dissolved, then set aside.

Turn the heat up under the wok as high as possible and add the groundnut oil. When the oil starts to smoke, add the garlic, chillies, lime leaves and galangal and stir-fry for 1 minute. Add the mushrooms and stir-fry for 10 minutes until all the moisture has cooked off and the mushrooms start to turn a golden colour. Add the shallots and sauce mixture and cook for a further minute, then transfer to a large bowl and leave to cool slightly. Add half the herbs and stir to combine.

To serve, set out the lettuce leaves on a platter to form cups and then divide the mushroom mixture between the lettuce cups. Sprinkle over the toasted rice powder and garnish with the remaining herbs. Serve with Thai sticky rice.

NOTE: You can make this with fresh shiitake mushrooms instead of King Oyster mushrooms, if you wish.

Kimchi Grilled Cheese Sandwich

**MAKES
2 SANDWICHES**

On the face of it, this may look like the sort of thing you'd knock up after getting back from the pub after a few too many beers, but for me this is proper comfort food. The sharp chilli-funk of fermented cabbage combined with nutty, melted cheese and buttery fried bread; snacks don't get much better than this.

4 slices of white bread
large spoonful of butter,
  softened
60g Cheddar, grated
60g Gruyère, grated
80g kimchi, drained and
  roughly chopped

Spread one side of each slice of bread with butter, then flip over and divide the grated cheeses equally between the slices. Top two of the slices with the kimchi, then sandwich together, pressing down to seal.

Heat a large frying pan over a medium heat, add the sandwiches and fry for 3–4 minutes on each side until the cheese is melted and the sandwiches are golden brown on the outside. Cut in half and devour.

NOTE: You can posh this up a bit by removing the crusts after cooking and slicing the sandwiches into fingers. But don't start using sourdough or anything fancy; this is the type of sandwich that needs simple sliced white.

Piquillo Pepper Jam

**MAKES
APPROXIMATELY
750G**

This is arguably the easiest condiment you'll ever make and has become a staple in our kitchen at home. I originally made this to serve with slices of Manchego cheese, but it goes with everything. It's delicious with cold meats or spooned over baked camembert, and keeps for ages in the fridge. Give the jars from the peppers a rinse and sterilise in a hot oven or in the dishwasher and they'll be ready to use by the time the jam has finished cooking.

500g jarred
  piquillo peppers
  (drained weight)
225g caster sugar
125ml cider vinegar
125ml water
½ teaspoon fine sea salt

Put all the ingredients in a food processor and pulse to a semi-smooth paste; it's nice to leave a bit of texture rather than blending to a completely smooth purée.

Pour the mixture into a stainless steel saucepan and bring to the boil, then reduce the heat and simmer gently for 30 minutes until thickened, stirring occasionally and skimming any scum from the surface. Remove the pan from the heat and leave to stand for 5 minutes.

Carefully pour the jam into sterilised jars, leave to cool and then seal. Store in a cool, dark place for up to 6 months.

Chargrilled Halloumi with Chilli and Mint Pesto

SERVES 4

Somewhat controversially, I'm not a huge fan of halloumi so the inclusion of this recipe may seem a little odd. It can often be bland and the texture either squeaky or chalky. However, I'm convinced there's a sweet spot; the moment it leaves the frying pan or griddle, with its golden, crisp exterior and salty, molten middle. Right there, in that almost-too-hot-to-eat moment, it's perfect. I hardly need say then that you need to make the pesto first so that you can dive straight in when the halloumi's ready.

750g halloumi, thickly
  sliced lengthways
olive oil
juice of ½ lemon

**FOR THE CHILLI
AND MINT PESTO:**
150ml light olive oil
75g pine nuts
2 red chillies, roughly
  chopped
1 small garlic clove,
  peeled and crushed
pinch of sea salt
50g bunch of mint,
  leaves picked
50g bunch of basil,
  leaves picked

First make the pesto. Pour the oil into a food processor, add the pine nuts, chillies, garlic and salt and blend to a coarse paste. Add the mint and basil leaves and blend again to a smooth paste.

Preheat a dry frying pan to a high heat. Brush the halloumi slices on both sides with a little olive oil, then chargrill for 2 minutes on each side until golden and lightly charred. Lay the chargrilled halloumi on a warmed serving plate, spoon over the pesto, then squeeze over the lemon juice and serve immediately.

NOTE: Buy the best halloumi you can lay your hands on (the good stuff's not expensive). Just like cheap mozzarella, cheap halloumi has little to no flavour and too firm a texture.

Agedashi Tofu

It's taken me a while to appreciate tofu; until recently I just didn't get it. Perhaps I'd only had poor quality stuff, but I'd always found it bland and, dare I say it, a bit pointless. But then I tasted agedashi and my previous opinions went out the window. Delicate, crispy and always served with a deeply savoury broth-like sauce, it was a bit of a revelation. I've always joked that things often taste better when deep-fried, but in this case it's true!

450g firm tofu
potato flour or cornflour,
   for dusting
vegetable oil,
   for deep-frying

FOR THE SAUCE:
20g dried kombu,
   rinsed
4 dried shiitake
   mushrooms, sliced
500ml water
2 tablespoons dark
   soy sauce
2 tablespoons mirin

TO SERVE:
10g dried wakame
   seaweed, soaked
   in water for about
   5 minutes and drained
50g mooli, peeled,
   finely grated and
   excess moisture
   squeezed out
3 spring onions,
   green parts only,
   finely chopped

Carefully unwrap the tofu and lay on a plate covered with five or six layers of kitchen paper. Cover with more kitchen paper, then lay a second plate on top. Leave to drain in the fridge for 2 hours.

Meanwhile, make the sauce. Put the kombu and mushrooms in a saucepan, pour over the cold water and slowly bring to the boil. Reduce the heat and simmer for 10 minutes, then strain into a jug. Pour 200ml of the stock into a bowl and stir in the soy sauce and mirin. Set aside. Any leftover stock can be frozen or stored in the fridge for up to 3 days and used as a base for soups or noodles.

Turn the tofu out onto a board and cut into 3cm cubes. Pour a deep layer of potato flour or cornflour onto a baking tray, add the cubes of tofu and gently roll each piece to coat evenly. Heat the vegetable oil in a deep fryer or large pan to 180°C. Fry the tofu, in batches, for 3–4 minutes until pale golden, removing from the oil and draining on kitchen paper as you go. Lastly, fry the wakame for 30 seconds until crisp; be careful, as it may splutter as it hits the hot oil. Remove from the oil and drain on kitchen paper.

Divide the tofu cubes between four small serving bowls and top each with a little grated mooli, spring onion greens and crispy wakame. Pour the sauce around the outside of the tofu and serve.

Som Tam Summer Rolls

MAKES 16

This recipe combines two of my favourite cuisines, Thai and Vietnamese. I've always loved Som Tam, the addictively spicy Thai green papaya salad, and Vietnamese summer rolls, translucent, chewy in a good way, and bursting with fresh herbs. This is messy food to be eaten with your hands, so don't spend ages making perfect parcels. Instead put a big bowl of the salad on the table with a stack of wrappers and the dipping sauce and let everyone roll their own.

1 garlic clove, peeled and crushed
2 red bird's-eye chillies, finely chopped
1 tablespoon palm sugar
juice of 2 limes
2 tablespoons No-fish Sauce (page 205)
100g fine green beans, trimmed and halved lengthways
8 cherry tomatoes, quartered
1 medium green papaya, peeled, deseeded and shredded
1 small bunch of Thai basil
1 small bunch of coriander
1 small bunch of mint
16 x 18cm round Vietnamese rice paper wrappers
100g dried rice noodles, soaked according to the packet instructions, refreshed under cold running water and drained

FOR THE PEANUT DIPPING SAUCE:
4 tablespoons crunchy peanut butter
1 tablespoon sriracha hot sauce
1 tablespoon dark soy sauce
juice of 1 lime
1 teaspoon palm sugar

Put the garlic, chillies, palm sugar, lime juice and No-fish Sauce in a large bowl and stir until the sugar has dissolved. Add the beans, tomatoes and papaya and toss to combine, then leave to stand for 10 minutes.

Meanwhile, put all the ingredients for the dipping sauce in a small bowl and stir to combine. Add a splash of boiling water to loosen the sauce to a dipping consistency, then set aside.

To assemble the rolls, lay a rice paper wrapper on a wooden board, then moisten with a clean, damp cloth until it softens enough to roll. Place a small mound of the salad along one edge of the wrapper, add a few leaves of each herb then top with a pinch of noodles. Fold the side of the wrapper into the middle, then roll away from you to seal. Repeat with the remaining wrappers and filling. Serve with the dipping sauce.

NOTE: Traditionally Som Tam ingredients are pounded, but I wanted to keep more crunch, so I've made it differently.

Steam-fried Buns

MAKES 24

This recipe is based on a combination of steamed *bao* buns and steam-fried *shuijian bao*. It's one of those recipes that can go in one of two directions; either pillowy, soft steamed buns, or golden, crispy buns with a light, steamed top. Whichever way you choose they'll be delicious and incredibly moreish. If you don't mind the extra washing up you could split the recipe and go for the best of both worlds.

FOR THE FILLING:
75g dried shiitake
  mushrooms
1 tablespoon groundnut
  oil or vegetable oil
30g fresh ginger,
  peeled and grated
6 spring onions,
  finely chopped
2 tablespoons dark
  soy sauce
1 tablespoon vegetarian
  oyster sauce
1 tablespoon cornflour
100g water chestnuts,
  finely chopped
pinch of white pepper

FOR THE DOUGH:
300g strong white
  bread flour
7g sachet fast-action
  dried yeast
2 teaspoons baking
  powder
2 tablespoons
  caster sugar
½ teaspoon fine sea salt
180ml warm water
3 tablespoons
  groundnut oil
  or vegetable oil,
  plus extra for oiling

First make the filling. Soak the dried mushrooms in boiling water for 15 minutes, then drain and leave to cool slightly. Remove and discard the stalks, then finely chop the caps. Heat the oil in a large frying pan over a high heat, add the chopped mushrooms and fry for 5 minutes. Add the ginger and spring onions and fry for a further couple of minutes. Whisk together the soy sauce, oyster sauce and cornflour in a small bowl until smooth, then pour into the pan. Stir everything together, cook, stirring, for 1 minute until thickened. Tip the filling mixture into a bowl and stir in the remaining ingredients. Cover and chill in the fridge for 30 minutes.

Divide the filling mixture into 24 equal-sized pieces; it may sound like a faff, but if you weigh the pieces of filling to make sure they're all the same, you will end up with even, perfectly cooked buns as a result. Roll each piece of filling into a ball.

For the dough, mix together the flour, yeast and baking powder in a large bowl. Add the sugar and salt to the water and stir until both have dissolved, then pour into the flour mixture with the oil and stir to form a dough. Tip the dough out onto a work surface and knead for 10 minutes until smooth and stretchy. Alternatively, you can use a stand mixer fitted with a dough hook to make this stage easier on your arms.

Divide the dough into 24 equal-sized pieces, weighing the pieces for accuracy as with the filling. Roll each piece of dough into a ball, then flatten each out into a thin round about 8cm in diameter. Place a ball of filling in the centre of each dough round, then gather the sides up and pinch together to seal. Flip the parcel over and press down to flatten slightly. Transfer the buns to a lightly oiled baking tray, cover with clingfilm and leave to rise at room temperature for 20 minutes.

CONTINUED OVERLEAF

Steam-fried Buns continued

Now here's where the recipe splits and you can either steam the buns or steam-fry them (or do both). The choice is yours.

TO STEAM THE BUNS: Cut small squares of greaseproof paper and stick one to the underside (i.e. the sealed side) of each bun. Sit the buns in a bamboo steamer, leaving a 3cm gap between each one to allow them to rise. Cover and steam for 8–10 minutes until risen. Take care when removing the steamer lid – tilt it away from you as you lift it to stop any condensation falling onto the tops of the buns, otherwise it will ruin their neat, shiny tops.

TO STEAM-FRY THE BUNS: You will need to do this in batches. Cover the base of a large, lidded frying pan with a thin coating of oil and set over a medium–high heat. Arrange the buns in the pan, again leaving a 3cm gap between each one to allow them to rise. As they start to sizzle, pour in enough boiling water to fill the base of the pan to a depth of about 1.5cm. Cover the pan, then cook for 8–10 minutes until the water has almost completely evaporated. Remove the lid and give the pan a gentle shake, then cook for a further few minutes until the base of the buns are golden and crisp. Flip over onto a serving plate so that the crispy sides are on top.

NOTE: Don't be tempted to halve the recipe as it doesn't really split easily. Instead make the full batch and freeze half. They cook perfectly from frozen – just add an extra minute to the cooking time.

Courgette Flowers with Ricotta and Black Pepper Honey

MAKES 12

Salty ricotta, floral honey and spicy black pepper are a match made in heaven, so bringing them together using sweet courgette flowers and crispy batter can only improve that union. If you grow courgettes, at some point you'll start to be overrun with flowers, but if not then keep an eye out for them in farmers' markets or befriend a neighbour with an allotment. Make sure that you pick out the bitter stamens from each flower and give them a shake to remove any bugs lurking within the folds of the petals. Don't be tempted to wash them in running water though; the petals are too delicate and will tear when you try to fill them.

12 courgette flowers
1 teaspoon crushed
  black peppercorns
4 tablespoons light
  floral honey
400g ricotta
80g Parmesan,
  finely grated
sea salt
vegetable oil,
  for deep-frying
75g self-raising flour
75g cornflour
175–200ml ice-cold
  sparkling water

First prepare the courgette flowers. Check them over for any small insects that may be hiding within the petals, then carefully pinch and twist the stamens and remove, as they tend to taste quite bitter.

Heat a small saucepan over a medium heat and lightly toast the crushed peppercorns until fragrant. Stir in the honey, then remove the pan from the heat and leave to infuse while you prepare the rest of the dish.

Beat together the ricotta and Parmesan in a bowl, then season to taste with salt. Spoon the mixture into a piping bag and pipe it into the courgette flowers until filled, then twist the tips of the petals together to seal.

Heat the vegetable oil in a deep fryer or large pan to 180°C. Combine the flours in a large bowl, add a good pinch of salt then make a well in the centre. Gradually whisk in enough sparkling water to make a smooth batter; it should be the consistency of double cream.

Dip the filled courgette flowers, a few at a time, into the batter to coat, shake off the excess and fry for 2 minutes until golden and crisp. Remove from the oil and drain on a plate lined with kitchen paper, then continue frying the remaining flowers in the same way. Sprinkle with a little salt, drizzle over the black pepper honey and serve.

IMAGE SHOWN OVERLEAF

Chargrilled Greens with Garlic Custard

**SERVES 4
AS A STARTER**

You'd be forgiven for thinking that 'garlic' and 'custard' are two words which shouldn't be used in the same sentence, let alone the same dish, so you'll just have to trust me. Blanching the garlic removes its strength and raw pungency, leaving you with a mellow, sweet flavour. This recipe originally started out as a dip for crispy pieces of grilled leaves, but then everything ended up in one bowl and it sort of morphed into something a little more refined. This makes a great starter, so have some crusty bread on hand to mop up the last vestiges of custard and scraps of charred leaves.

6 garlic cloves, peeled
200ml whole milk
5 medium egg yolks
200ml double cream
sea salt and
  white pepper
400g mixed greens
  such as cavolo nero,
  mustard greens,
  broccoli leaves and
  cauliflower leaves,
  leaves separated
  and roughly torn
rapeseed oil
juice of ½ lemon

Put the garlic cloves in a saucepan, cover with cold water and bring to the boil. Drain, then repeat this process a further two times. Put the blanched garlic back in the saucepan, cover with the milk and bring to a gentle simmer. Whisk the egg yolks and cream together, then pour into the pan. Cook gently, stirring constantly, until the custard has thickened then pour into a liquidiser and leave to cool slightly. Blend until smooth, season to taste then set aside to cool to room temperature. Divide between four serving bowls.

Preheat a barbecue or cast-iron griddle pan to a high heat. Brush the leaves with a little rapeseed oil, then chargrill, turning regularly, for 2–3 minutes or until lightly charred and just starting to wilt. More robust leaves may take slightly longer, whereas younger, softer leaves take hardly any time at all. The trick is to cook them hard and fast so that they char yet retain a bit of crunch.

Drizzle the leaves with the lemon juice, season with salt and immediately pile on top of the garlic custard and serve.

Fried Baby Artichokes with Aioli and Smoked Cheese

SERVES 4

I have a bit of a love-hate relationship with artichokes; I love to eat them, but find them a pain to prepare (which is why I often order them when eating out as someone else has done all the hard work). Baby artichokes, however, are much easier. Their fibrous chokes haven't developed enough to warrant removal, so they're far less fiddly and just as delicious. Be warned, this is quite a rich dish so you'll need plenty of chilled dry white wine to wash it down.

12 baby artichokes
250ml buttermilk
sea salt and freshly
    ground black pepper
vegetable oil,
    for deep-frying
125g plain flour
25g cornflour

FOR THE AIOLI:
1 medium egg yolk
1 fat garlic clove,
    peeled and crushed
½ teaspoon mustard
    powder
good pinch of sea salt
100ml vegetable oil
25ml extra virgin
    rapeseed oil
squeeze of lemon juice,
    to taste

100g smoked hard
    cheese (I use smoked
    Lincolnshire Poacher
    or Cheddar), to serve

Trim the tough outer leaves from each artichoke, leaving the pale yellow-green heart exposed. Using a potato peeler, peel the outer layer from the stalk, then cut each artichoke in half lengthways. Combine with the buttermilk in a large bowl and plenty of salt and black pepper, then leave to stand for 10 minutes.

Meanwhile, make the aioli. Put the egg yolk, garlic and mustard powder in a separate large bowl, add the salt and whisk together until smooth. Combine the oils in a jug and, whisking constantly, begin to pour the oil into the bowl in a very thin, steady stream. It's crucial that you really take your time at this stage; over-zealous oil pouring will result in splitting. Continue steadily adding the oil, still whisking constantly, until it's all incorporated. Whisk in the lemon juice to taste; it needs to be fairly sharp to cut through the richness of the artichokes and cheese.

Heat the vegetable oil in a deep fryer or a large pan to 180°C. Tip the plain flour and cornflour into another large bowl and season with salt and black pepper. Shake the excess buttermilk from the artichokes, then drop them into the seasoned flour and toss to coat. Shake off the excess flour, then deep-fry the artichokes, a few at a time, for 4–5 minutes until deep golden and crisp. Remove from the oil and drain on kitchen paper, then season straight away with a pinch of salt.

Arrange the artichokes on a large plate, then use a potato peeler to shave the smoked cheese over the top. Serve with the aioli for dipping.

Flatbreads with Creamed Feta and Sticky Aubergines

SERVES 4

Pillowy soft, lightly charred flatbreads piled high with toppings are a great way to start a meal, particularly if you're feeding a crowd. I tend to make both the pickled carrots and the sticky aubergines, put everything in the middle of the table and let everyone dive in. These also make a great main course; double the recipe and serve with larger flatbreads, barbecued lamb or veggies and a simple herb salad.

1 garlic clove, peeled and crushed
2 teaspoons ground sumac, plus extra to serve
2 tablespoons extra virgin olive oil, plus extra to serve
sea salt
100g feta, crumbled
75ml double cream
50g cream cheese

FOR THE CARROTS:
150ml white wine vinegar
100ml water
1 tablespoon caster sugar
1 tablespoon yellow mustard seeds
2 large carrots, peeled and cut into thin matchsticks
1 teaspoon sea salt flakes

FOR THE STICKY AUBERGINES:
olive oil
2 medium aubergines, cut into 2cm cubes
2 teaspoons cumin seeds, lightly crushed
1 tablespoon dark brown soft sugar
3 tablespoons sherry vinegar

4 thick white flatbreads, to serve
zaatar, to serve

Whisk together the garlic, sumac, oil and a pinch of salt, then leave to infuse. Put the feta in a small food processor and blend to a fine crumb consistency. With the motor running, gradually add the cream and blend until smooth. Add the cream cheese and blend again until thickened. Tip into a bowl, cover and chill.

Combine the vinegar, water, sugar and mustard seeds in a saucepan. Bring to the boil then simmer for 10 minutes. Put the carrots into a large bowl with the salt then gently work everything together with your hands. Gently knead the carrots for 5 minutes until they've softened and start to release liquid. Pour over the vinegar mixture then leave to cool to room temperature. Drain through a fine sieve, making sure you keep the mustard seeds.

Meanwhile, heat a little olive oil in a large frying pan, add one quarter of the aubergines and fry over a high heat for 5 minutes until softened and caramelised. Tip onto a plate lined with kitchen paper and squeeze to remove as much excess oil as possible. Repeat with the remaining aubergines, then return all of it to the pan. Add the cumin seeds and sugar and fry for a couple of minutes. Pour over the vinegar and continue to cook over a high heat until all the vinegar has been absorbed and the aubergines are dark and sticky. Season to taste with salt.

When you're ready to serve, heat a heavy-based griddle pan over a high heat and lightly toast the flatbreads until warmed through. Brush with the infused oil, then spread generously with the creamed feta. Spoon the pickled carrots or aubergine on top and finish with a drizzle of olive oil and sprinkle of zaatar and sumac.

Banh Xeo

SERVES 4

These light, lacy pancakes encompass everything I love about Vietnamese food; crisp, crunchy textures and an abundance of fiery chilli and fresh herbs. The batter needs to be made at least 2 hours in advance but really benefits from being chilled overnight. As an added bonus they're also gluten and dairy free.

FOR THE BATTER:
100g rice flour
1 tablespoon cornflour
1 teaspoon
   ground turmeric
pinch of fine sea salt
200ml coconut milk
150–200ml cold water

FOR THE NUOC CHAM SAUCE:
juice of 2 limes
3 tablespoons water
2 tablespoons No-fish
   Sauce (page 205)
1 tablespoon
   caster sugar
1 Thai red chilli,
   finely sliced
1 garlic clove, peeled
   and finely chopped

FOR THE FILLING:
vegetable oil
1 onion, peeled
   and thinly sliced
4 large Portobello
   mushrooms,
   thickly sliced
1 tablespoon dark
   soy sauce
120g beansprouts
2 spring onions,
   finely sliced
1 tablespoon crushed
   roasted peanuts
1 small bunch of
   coriander, leaves picked
1 small bunch of mint,
   leaves picked
1 small bunch of Thai
   basil, leaves picked
1 Batavia or Romaine
   lettuce, leaves separated

Start by making the batter. Sift the rice flour, cornflour, turmeric and salt into a large bowl and make a well in the middle. Whisk in the coconut milk then gradually whisk in enough water until you have a smooth, thin batter; it should just coat the back of the spoon and be roughly the consistency of pouring cream. Cover the bowl with clingfilm and chill in the fridge for at least 2 hours, or overnight if you have time.

When you're ready to cook the pancakes, put all the ingredients for the sauce into a small bowl and stir until the sugar has dissolved. Now get all the herbs and other filling ingredients ready so that you can stuff the pancakes as soon as they're fried.

Heat a splash of vegetable oil in a wok over a high heat until smoking. Add the onion and fry for a couple of minutes until lightly charred and beginning to soften. Add the mushrooms and fry, still over a high heat, for 5 minutes until caramelised; the idea here is to drive off as much moisture as possible to avoid soggy pancakes. Season with the soy sauce and cook for a couple of minutes until all the liquid in the pan has been absorbed. Tip the mushrooms and onion onto a warmed plate in a single layer; if you pile them up, they will start to sweat.

Heat a little more oil in a non-stick frying pan over a medium heat, give the batter a quick whisk and then pour in enough to coat the base of the pan in a thin layer. The pancake should quickly start to turn lacy, with tiny holes around the outer edge. Continue to cook for a minute or so until the surface of the batter is quite dry. Top with a handful of the mushroom and onion mixture and beansprouts, then scatter over a little spring onion and a few peanuts. Slide the pancake onto a plate and then repeat with the remaining batter and filling ingredients.

Serve the pancakes warm with the herbs and lettuce for stuffing, and the sauce for dipping.

MAINS

Whipped Yellow Peas with Spicy Aubergine and Fennel

SERVES 4

The trick to this dish is not overcooking the aubergines. They need to be just cooked through so that they're fairly soft, but still holding their shape. If you take them too far you won't get the contrast in texture between them and the silky smooth peas. A cautionary note about harissa; the level of heat varies greatly depending on where you buy it (the supermarket stuff tends to be more gentle, whereas the Tunisian variety in tubes is pretty fiery stuff). With that in mind, add it gradually and to taste.

FOR THE SPLIT PEAS:
350g dried yellow
    split peas
1 teaspoon ground
    turmeric
3 garlic cloves, peeled
1 teaspoon fine sea salt
750ml Vegetable Stock
    (page 200)
3 tablespoons extra
    virgin olive oil

**FOR THE SPICY
AUBERGINE:**
4 medium aubergines
olive oil, for frying
3 garlic cloves,
    peeled and crushed
2 teaspoons
    cumin seeds
3 tablespoons
    tomato purée
1–2 tablespoons
    harissa paste
450ml Vegetable Stock
    (page 200)
2 teaspoons red wine
    vinegar

FOR THE FENNEL:
1 large fennel bulb
pinch of sea salt
juice of ½ lemon

Rinse the split peas, then leave them to soak in cold water for 1 hour. Drain, then tip into a heavy-based saucepan with the turmeric, garlic and salt. Pour over the stock and bring to the boil, then reduce the heat, cover with a lid and simmer gently for 1 hour until almost all the liquid has been absorbed.

Meanwhile, prepare the spicy aubergine. Cut each aubergine widthways into thirds, then slice each piece into wedges. Heat a splash of oil in a deep frying pan and fry, in batches, over a medium heat for about 10 minutes until golden, transferring to a plate lined with kitchen paper as you go. Return all the aubergine to the pan, then increase the heat, add the garlic and fry for 2 minutes. Sprinkle in the cumin seeds and fry for a further minute, then add the tomato purée and harissa to taste and fry for 2 minutes. Pour over the stock – it will bubble up viciously at this point, so stand back to avoid getting splattered – and cook for 3–4 minutes until the liquid has mostly been absorbed. Remove from the heat and stir in the vinegar.

Thinly slice the fennel on a mandolin or using a very sharp knife, then toss with the salt in a bowl. Massage the fennel for a minute or so until it begins to soften slightly, then squeeze over the lemon juice.

Pour the cooked split peas into a liquidiser, add the extra virgin olive oil and blend to a smooth purée – add a little water if it needs some encouragement. Pour into a clean pan and set aside.

To serve, gently reheat the split pea purée, divide between warmed serving bowls, spoon over the spicy aubergine and top with the fennel.

Orecchiette with Walnut Pesto and Broccoli

SERVES 4

I love making pesto; you can't beat the heady aniseed scent of basil filling your kitchen and it tastes infinitely better than anything you can buy in the shops. This version, *pesto di noci*, uses walnuts instead of pine nuts, giving the sauce a robust bitterness. Purists will say that proper pesto should only be made by hand using a pestle and mortar, but sometimes life's too short to be pure. If you've got a decent food processor it'll make it in a fraction of the time and I challenge you to notice the difference.

150g walnut halves
1 small garlic clove,
    peeled
pinch of sea salt flakes
200g basil leaves
100–120ml olive oil
35g pecorino,
    finely grated,
    plus extra to serve
400g dried orecchiette
400g Tenderstem
    broccoli

Preheat the oven to 180°C/gas mark 4. Spread the walnuts out on a roasting tray and roast for 10 minutes. Tip out onto a clean tea towel and use it to rub the nuts and gently remove the skins. Don't worry about being too fastidious; as long as some of the skins are removed, the pesto won't taste too bitter.

Pulse the garlic, salt and two thirds of the walnuts in a food processor to a rough crumb consistency. Throw in the basil leaves and oil then blend to a smooth paste. Stir in the cheese and taste, adding a little more salt if you feel the need.

Bring a large pan of salted water to the boil, add the orecchiette and cook according to the packet instructions; I always cook dried pasta for 1 minute less than it says on the packet to keep it al dente. While the pasta is cooking, separate the broccoli stalks from the heads and then thinly slice. Add the sliced broccoli stalks to the pan 3 minutes before the pasta is ready, then the broccoli heads for the final 2 minutes of cooking. Drain and tip the pasta and broccoli into a large, warmed bowl, add the pesto and toss to coat.

To serve, divide the pasta mixture between four warmed serving bowls, crush the remaining walnuts over the top and finish with a little grated pecorino.

Spinach and Blue Cheese Polenta with Slow-roasted Tomatoes

SERVES 4

This dish relies on just a few simple ingredients and plenty of time. The tomatoes are the real star of the show and can't be rushed; the only way to sticky, jammy sweetness is through low, slow roasting. You could use quick-cook polenta, but why bother when there's no rush? You have to wait for the tomatoes, so you may as well use the long-cook variety which has a far better flavour and texture. This is Sunday afternoon cooking at its best, so take your time, put your feet up and it will be worth the wait.

3 tablespoons extra virgin olive oil
2 garlic cloves, peeled and crushed
sea salt
500g baby San Marzano or baby plum tomatoes, halved lengthways

FOR THE SPINACH AND BLUE CHEESE POLENTA:
600g large-leaf spinach, washed and stalks removed
1.2 litres Vegetable Stock (page 200)
200g polenta
40g unsalted butter, cubed
60g Parmesan, finely grated
150g Dolcelatte Piccante or Roquefort, diced

Preheat the oven to 120°C/gas mark ½. Line a baking tray with greaseproof paper.

Whisk together the oil, garlic and a pinch of salt in a large bowl, add the tomatoes and toss to coat. Arrange the tomatoes, cut-side up, on the lined tray and roast for 2 hours until soft and sticky.

For the polenta, bring a large pan of water to the boil, add the spinach leaves and cook for 1–2 minutes until wilted. Drain thoroughly, then squeeze dry using plenty of kitchen paper. Roughly chop and set aside.

Pour the stock into the spinach pan and bring to the boil, then whisk in the polenta, ensuring that you whisk constantly to prevent the polenta from turning lumpy. Reduce the heat and cook slowly, stirring regularly, for 30–35 minutes until the polenta has thickened and starts to pull away from the sides of the pan. Remove the pan from the heat, whisk in the butter and Parmesan and then fold in the spinach and blue cheese.

Divide the polenta between four warmed serving bowls and top with the sticky roasted tomatoes.

IMAGE SHOWN ON PREVIOUS PAGE

Greek Stuffed Tomatoes

I love our holidays in Greece; lazy days on the beach followed by long dinners in local tavernas, the food and wine simple and delicious. These stuffed tomatoes appear on every menu and are really easy to replicate at home. They are even better made a day ahead as the rice firms up slightly and the flavours really develop overnight. Just reheat in the oven until piping hot.

4 large beef tomatoes
olive oil
1 onion, peeled
  and finely chopped
2 garlic cloves,
  peeled and crushed
1 tablespoon
  tomato purée
1 teaspoon
  dried oregano
½ teaspoon dried mint
a handful of pitted
  Kalamata olives,
  chopped
100ml dry white wine
1 tablespoon
  red wine vinegar
100g long-grain
  white rice
100g feta, crumbled
sea salt and
  black pepper

FOR THE SALAD:
½ cucumber,
  peeled, deseeded
  and chopped
pinch of dried chilli flakes
2 teaspoons
  red wine vinegar
1 tablespoon
  extra virgin olive oil
1 small bunch of mint,
  leaves picked, torn

Preheat the oven to 160°C/gas mark 3. Cut the tops off the tomatoes, then use a spoon to scoop out the flesh from each. Finely chop the flesh and set aside.

Heat a splash of olive oil in a saucepan, add the onion and fry gently for 10 minutes until softened and caramelised. Add the garlic and fry for a couple of minutes, then stir in the tomato purée and dried herbs and cook until the mixture turns a deep red colour. Stir in the chopped tomato flesh, the olives, wine and vinegar. Bring to a simmer and cook for 5 minutes until the tomatoes have softened and reduced slightly. Stir in the rice and cook for 5 minutes; the rice should be soft around the edges but still firm in the middle of the grain. Fold the feta through the rice mixture and season to taste with salt and black pepper; it shouldn't need much salt as the olives and feta will do the job.

Spoon the rice mixture into the tomato shells and put the tops back on. Sit the tomatoes in a roasting tray, drizzle with olive oil and cover with foil. Bake for 1 hour, then remove the foil and bake for a further 15 minutes.

Meanwhile, mix together the ingredients for the salad in a bowl and season to taste with salt and black pepper.

Spoon any roasting juices over the tomatoes and then serve with the salad.

IMAGE SHOWN OVERLEAF

Butternut Squash Laksa

SERVES 4

It may seem like a daunting list of ingredients, but this fragrant spiced noodle soup is surprisingly easy to make and is ready in a little more than 30 minutes. If you're making a special trip to buy the ingredients for this recipe, I'd suggest making a double batch of the paste and freezing half for use another time. A good laksa should be piping hot, vibrant and fresh, so serve it the moment it's ready.

1 butternut squash,
  approximately 1kg
3 tablespoons coconut
  oil or vegetable oil
400g can coconut milk
1.2 litres Vegetable Stock
  (page 200)
2 tablespoons No-fish
  Sauce (page 205)
1 tablespoon
  palm sugar
juice of 1–2 limes,
  to taste
200g dried
  rice noodles

FOR THE PASTE:
3 dried red chillies,
  deseeded
30g piece of fresh
  ginger, peeled
  and chopped
3 shallots,
  peeled and chopped
4 garlic cloves,
  peeled and crushed
3 Thai red chillies,
  deseeded and chopped
2 lemongrass stalks,
  outer tough layers
  removed, chopped
6 lime leaves,
  stems removed
2 teaspoons
  ground coriander
2 teaspoons
  ground cumin
3 tablespoons
  vegetable oil
2 teaspoons
  ground turmeric

TO SERVE:
200g beansprouts
4 tablespoons roasted
  peanuts, crushed
1 Thai red chilli,
  finely sliced
1 small bunch of mint,
  leaves picked and torn
1 small bunch of
  coriander, leaves picked
  and torn
1 small bunch of Thai
  basil, leaves picked
  and torn
lime wedges

Preheat the oven to 180°C/gas mark 4. Line a roasting tray with greaseproof paper. Cut the squash in half through the middle. Peel the thick stem section and cut into 2cm cubes. Toss in 2 tablespoons of the oil, tip into the lined roasting tray and roast for 30 minutes until tender. Remove from the oven and set aside. Peel, deseed and coarsely grate the remaining squash.

For the paste, put all the ingredients, except the turmeric (which has a habit of staining everything), into a small food processor and blend until smooth.

Heat the remaining tablespoon of oil in a large saucepan over a medium heat. Add the paste with the turmeric, and fry, stirring, for 2–3 minutes until fragrant. Add the grated squash and fry for a further 2 minutes. Pour in the coconut milk and stock and bring to the boil, then reduce the heat and simmer for 10 minutes until the squash has softened. Remove the pan from the heat and stir in the lime leaves, No-fish Sauce, palm sugar and lime juice to taste. Leave to cool slightly, then pour into a liquidiser and blend until smooth. Return to the pan and keep warm.

Meanwhile, soak the noodles in boiling water for 10 minutes, then drain, rinse under cold running water and drain again.

To serve, divide the noodles, roast squash and beansprouts between four warmed serving bowls. Pour the soup over the top, then sprinkle with the peanuts, sliced chilli and herbs. Serve with lime wedges.

Artichoke and Lemon Orzo Risotto

SERVES 4

This isn't strictly a risotto as it uses pasta in place of rice, but it tastes just as good and requires far less effort. A rice-based risotto needs to be stirred constantly to release the starch and achieve a creamy texture, but pasta can just be left to simmer away with little attention. There's a time and a place for fresh artichokes, but this isn't one of them; jarred work perfectly well here and the flavoured oil makes a great starting point for adding flavour to the base.

350g sliced artichokes
 in oil, drained and oil
 reserved
20g butter
1 shallot, peeled
 and finely chopped
1 garlic clove, peeled
 and crushed
350g dried orzo pasta
150ml dry white wine
1 litre hot Vegetable
 Stock (page 200)

TO FINISH:
25g cold butter, cubed
50g Parmesan,
 finely grated,
 plus extra to serve
finely grated zest
 of 1 unwaxed lemon

Lemon Oil (page 203),
 to serve

Heat 2 tablespoons of the reserved artichoke oil with the butter in a shallow, heavy-based saucepan over a medium heat. Add the shallot and garlic and fry for 3 minutes until soft. Add the orzo and fry, stirring, for 1 minute.

Pour in the wine and bring to the boil, then leave to bubble away for a minute or so to burn off the alcohol. Add a ladleful of the hot stock and cook over a medium heat, stirring, until almost all the stock has been absorbed, then pour in the remaining stock and continue to cook for 10 minutes. Stir the pasta occasionally but not constantly as you would a rice-based risotto as you'll release too much starch.

Remove the pan from the heat and beat in the cold butter, Parmesan and lemon zest. Stir through the artichokes and serve topped with a little extra grated Parmesan and a drizzle of Lemon Oil.

Cavatelli with Trompettes and Cavolo Nero

SERVES 2

Just like the Singapore Noodles (page 94), some dishes are best made in smaller quantities and simply don't scale up that easily. By working with fewer ingredients in the pan, things don't get crowded; the mushrooms stay bouncy, the cavolo nero doesn't stew and the result is firm pasta coated in a silky sauce with crisp vegetables. The poached egg yolk binds everything together, but it's not crucial and can be left out if you'd prefer. I use trompette mushrooms as I love the texture, but any mix of dried wild mushrooms will do; they're easily available and lend a certain woodland flavour to dishes.

20g dried trompette
  mushrooms
fine sea salt
200g dried
  cavatelli pasta
1 tablespoon olive oil
20g butter
2 garlic cloves,
  peeled and crushed
200g cavolo nero
  (black kale), stalks
  removed (see page
  133), leaves chopped
40g Parmesan,
  finely grated,
  plus extra to serve
freshly ground black
  pepper
2 medium egg yolks,
  left whole

Soak the dried mushrooms in boiling water for 20 minutes, then drain and pat dry with kitchen paper.

Bring a large pan of salted water to the boil, add the pasta and cook for 10 minutes.

Meanwhile, heat the oil and butter in a separate pan large enough to accommodate the cooked pasta. Add the mushrooms and garlic and fry for 5 minutes until softened. Add the cavolo nero and fry for a couple of minutes, then add a splash of the pasta cooking water.

Drain the pasta, reserving the cooking water, then add the pasta to the mushroom pan. Toss everything together, gradually adding the Parmesan and a little extra pasta water until everything is coated in a light, silky sauce. Season with plenty of black pepper, then divide between two warmed serving bowls.

Lower the egg yolks into the still-hot pasta water with a slotted spoon, leave them for 1 minute, then carefully remove. Top each bowl of pasta with an egg yolk and finish with a little extra Parmesan.

Chilli Paneer

The first time I tasted just how good this dish could be was when my wife and I were travelling around Rajasthan. We were staying in Udaipur and were taken to a tiny place on the edge of a busy road. There were no tables so we sat on upturned beer crates and balanced hot plates of paneer on our knees alongside motorbikes and cars whizzing past just a couple of feet away. The flavour was incredible; the sauce was fiery and full of black pepper and the paneer beautifully crisp. This is a dish that needs to be made and served quickly to keep everything vibrant and stop the batter from turning soggy.

2 tablespoons
  plain flour
2 tablespoons
  cornflour
1 teaspoon
  Sichuan peppercorns,
  crushed
1 tablespoon dark
  soy sauce
3–4 tablespoons whole
  milk
pinch of fine sea salt
vegetable oil,
  for deep-frying
200g block of paneer,
  cut into 12 cubes
  and patted dry

FOR THE SAUCE:
3 tablespoons water
2 tablespoons white
  wine vinegar
2 tablespoons
  tomato ketchup
2 tablespoons dark
  soy sauce
2–3 tablespoons
  chilli sauce, depending
  on how hot you like it
1 teaspoon cornflour

FOR THE STIR-FRY:
1 tablespoon
  vegetable oil
1 onion, peeled
  and cut into large dice
1 green pepper,
  deseeded and cut
  into large dice
3 garlic cloves,
  peeled and crushed
2 green chillies,
  finely chopped
a thumb-sized piece
  of fresh ginger,
  peeled and grated
1 teaspoon Sichuan
  peppercorns, crushed
½ teaspoon crushed
  black peppercorns

To make the batter, whisk together the plain flour, cornflour, Sichuan peppercorns, soy sauce, milk and salt in a large bowl until smooth. Set aside to rest.

Whisk together the ingredients for the sauce in a small bowl and keep them near the hob.

Heat the vegetable oil for deep-frying in a large pan or deep-fat fryer to 180°C. Add the paneer cubes to the batter and toss to coat. Take a handful of cubes, shake off the excess batter and deep-fry for 2–3 minutes until golden and crisp. Remove from the oil and drain on a plate lined with kitchen paper, then continue deep-frying the remaining paneer cubes in the same way.

For the stir-fry, heat a large wok over a high heat, pour in the vegetable oil and heat until it begins to smoke. Add the onion and green pepper and stir-fry for 3 minutes until softened and lightly charred. Add the garlic, chillies, ginger and all the peppercorns and stir-fry for a further 2 minutes. Pour in the sauce and let everything bubble for a couple of minutes. Add the deep-fried paneer cubes and toss to coat, then tip the stir-fry straight into warmed serving bowls. This is a dish best eaten as hot as you can handle so that you get the contrast between the silky sauce and crunchy deep-fried paneer. If you leave it to sit for too long, the batter will turn soggy, and although it will still be delicious, this dish is all about that crunch.

Smoked Mushroom Ramen

Ramen has soared in popularity in recent years and it's easy to see why; it's flavourful, comforting and offers endless variety. The key to a good ramen is the broth; it needs to be clean, rich and packed with flavour. In the absence of meat bones, I make mine with mushrooms and seaweed as both are naturally rich in flavour-boosting MSG. Smoking the mushrooms adds an extra layer of flavour, but if it's too much work (or likely to land you in trouble) then you can skip this step. I always think that serving ramen is the perfect opportunity to be a bit creative and really show off the ingredients, then everyone can mix them in as they slurp away.

FOR THE BROTH:
2.5 litres Vegetable Stock (page 200)
20 dried shiitake mushrooms
1 bunch of spring onions, roughly chopped
10 x 10cm piece of dried kombu, rinsed
1 tablespoon mirin
2 tablespoons light soy sauce

FOR THE RAMEN:
480g dried ramen noodles (4 x 120g nests)
1 head of spring greens, finely shredded
150g enoki or shimeji mushrooms
150g bamboo shoots

TO SERVE:
4 medium poached eggs
4 spring onions, thinly sliced

You will need a small handful of cedar, oak or apple wood smoking chips

For the broth, pour the stock into a large saucepan, add the shiitake mushrooms and spring onions and bring to a gentle simmer. Cover the pan and cook gently for 20 minutes. Add the kombu and simmer for a further 10 minutes, then remove the pan from the heat. Strain the stock into a clean pan and discard the spring onions and kombu, reserving the shiitake mushrooms. Season the broth with the mirin and 1 tablespoon of the soy sauce and set aside.

Remove the stalks from the shiitake and discard, then thickly slice the caps and toss them in the remaining tablespoon of soy sauce.

Now for the messy part. Open your kitchen windows and crank up your oven extractor fan. Put the wood chips in the bottom of a stainless steel pan and set over a high heat until they blacken and begin to smoulder; you can speed the process up by using a chef's blowtorch if you have one. Set a metal steamer basket on top of the wood chips and arrange the mushroom slices on top. Cover with a lid and leave for a minute, then remove the pan from the heat. Set the pan and steamer aside, with the lid on, and leave the mushrooms to smoke gently for 30 minutes. Meanwhile, get the remaining ingredients ready to assemble.

For the ramen, bring a pan of water to the boil, add the noodles and cook according to the packet instructions. Drain and divide between four warmed deep serving bowls.

Bring the broth to a gentle simmer, add the smoked mushrooms and reheat gently. Add the spring greens, enoki or shimeji mushrooms and bamboo shoots and bring back to a simmer. Divide the broth and vegetables between the serving bowls, top each with a poached egg and finish with the spring onions.

Leek and Potato Soup

SERVES 4

My Granny was a fantastic cook and would make everything from scratch, only consulting books or saved scraps of paper if she needed to jog her memory about some small detail. Whenever we went to visit, we'd always joke that we wouldn't get out of the car until we knew that she had a batch of her famous leek and potato soup ready (and her even more famous chocolate ice cream in the freezer). Of course, she never disappointed. This is my version of her soup, using all of the same quantities and ingredients, but just 'poshed up' slightly. I like to think she'd have enjoyed eating this then quietly tutted and said that hers was better (and she'd be right).

400g Charlotte potatoes
500g leeks
    (3 medium leeks),
    trimmed, washed
    thoroughly and
    patted dry
50g unsalted butter
750ml Vegetable Stock
    (page 200)
vegetable oil, for frying
150g baby leaf spinach,
    washed
sea salt and white
    pepper

Peel the potatoes, then trim into rectangles and cut into 1cm dice. Finely chop the potato trimmings and most of the leeks, reserving one third of the white part of one of the leeks.

Heat the butter in a saucepan until foaming, add the leeks and potato trimmings and fry gently for 7–8 minutes, stirring regularly.

Meanwhile, bring the stock to the boil in a separate saucepan, add the potato cubes and simmer for 10 minutes until softened but still holding their shape. Drain the potato cubes, reserving the stock (and cubes), and set aside.

Pour the stock into the pan with the leeks and bring to the boil, then reduce the heat and simmer for 5 minutes until the potato trimmings are soft.

Meanwhile, cut the reserved piece of leek in half lengthways and then finely shred. Put the leek into a small pan, cover with vegetable oil and set over a medium–high heat. Stir the leek with a fork so that it's moved around the pan and cooked evenly. The leeks are ready when they have turned a pale golden colour and the bubbles in the oil subside. Remove from the pan and drain on kitchen paper.

Pour the stock mixture into a liquidiser, add the spinach and blend until smooth. Season to taste with salt and white pepper.

To serve, divide the potato between four warmed serving bowls, pour over the soup and top with the crispy leeks.

Celeriac Soup with Candied Pecans

SERVES 4

It was always my intention to avoid any 'meat replacement' recipes when writing this book, but inevitably there would be a few exceptions. I'd usually top this soup with pieces of crispy smoked bacon and without them it seemed to be somewhat lacking. Cue then, the candied pecans; salty, sweet, smoky and with a hint of clove, they really do taste like nuggets of crispy bacon. This soup is autumn in a bowl; creamy, earthy and perfect fodder for warming the cockles after a long walk in the woods, kicking through piles of fallen leaves.

800g celeriac,
  peeled and cut into
  2cm chunks
750ml Vegetable Stock
  (page 200)
250ml whole milk
sea salt and white
  pepper

FOR THE CANDIED PECANS:
50g caster sugar
½ teaspoon
  smoked paprika
¼ teaspoon
  ground cinnamon
¼ teaspoon
  sea salt flakes
pinch of dried chilli flakes
pinch of ground cloves
50g pecans,
  crumbled

Put the celeriac in a saucepan, pour over the stock and milk and bring to the boil. Reduce the heat and simmer for 20 minutes or until the celeriac is soft, stirring every now and then; it should give easily when pressed against the side of the pan with a spoon.

Meanwhile, prepare the candied pecans. Line a baking tray with greaseproof paper. Heat the sugar in a non-stick frying pan over a medium heat until melted; keep tilting and swirling the pan so that the sugar cooks evenly. As the sugar starts to turn a light golden colour, tip in the spices and pecans and stir with a heatproof rubber spatula. Give the nuts a further minute over the heat, then tip onto the lined tray, spread out in an even layer and leave to cool.

Remove the soup pan from the heat and leave the soup to cool slightly, then pour into a liquidiser and blend until smooth. Season to taste with salt and white pepper. Pour the soup into warmed serving bowls and scatter over the candied pecans.

Gnocchi with Caponata and Burrata Cream

SERVES 4

This recipe is my version of a delicious dish that I ate at a Florentine restaurant called *Il Santo Bevitore*. It's one of the best restaurants I've ever eaten at — one where clever cooking using the very finest, yet simple, ingredients makes a truly memorable meal. Everything we ate there was incredible, but this one dish really stood out.

FOR THE GNOCCHI:
fine salt
500g Désirée potatoes,
   peeled and quartered
100g '00' pasta flour,
   plus extra for dusting
1 medium egg, beaten
fine semolina,
   for dusting the tray
splash of olive oil,
   for oiling and frying
large knob of butter

FOR THE BURRATA CREAM:
200g burrata
2 tablespoons extra
   virgin olive oil
pinch of sea salt

TO SERVE:
½ quantity of Caponata
   (page 30)
grated Parmesan

For the gnocchi, bring a large pan of water to the boil and salt it generously. Add the potatoes, reduce the heat and simmer for 25–30 minutes until tender. Drain thoroughly, then arrange the potatoes on a wire rack and leave to steam for 5 minutes.

Meanwhile, make the burrata cream. Pat the cheese dry with kitchen paper. Tear into chunks, then put in a liquidiser with the oil and salt and blend for 4–5 minutes. The mixture will eventually thicken, and once it has reached the consistency of mayonnaise, stop blending and spoon into a bowl. Set aside at room temperature.

Press the cooked potatoes through a sieve into a large bowl. Add the flour, then very gently knead together, adding the egg gradually. As soon as the mixture comes together to form a soft dough, turn out onto a lightly floured work surface. Divide it into four equal pieces, then roll each piece into a sausage shape about 1.5cm thick. Dust a baking tray with fine semolina. Using a floured knife, cut the dough 'sausages' into 1.5cm lengths and transfer to the prepared tray. Shake the tray occasionally to stop the gnocchi from sticking together.

Bring a large pan of salted water to the boil, and lightly oil a tray. Cook the gnocchi in batches, for about 30 seconds at a time. They're ready as soon as they float to the surface. Transfer the cooked gnocchi to the oiled tray using a small sieve and leave to cool slightly.

Heat a splash of oil in a large frying pan over a high heat and add the gnocchi. Fry for a couple of minutes, then add the butter and cook for a further minute until deep golden. Drain on a tray lined with kitchen paper.

Reheat the caponata, then divide the burrata cream between four warmed serving bowls. Top with the gnocchi, spoon over the caponata and finish with Parmesan.

SERVES 4

Porcini Risotto

A fat, fresh porcini mushroom is a wonderful thing, but unless you're a forager it's also a rare and expensive one. Thankfully the dried variety are relatively wallet-friendly and have the added bonus of being useful for infusing the all-important stock with plenty of fungi flavour. If, however, you do manage to get hold of some fresh porcini, then follow the recipe below and top with some thick slices fried in butter until golden.

30g dried porcini
   mushrooms
1 litre hot Vegetable
   Stock (page 200)
50g Parmesan,
   finely grated
70g butter
olive oil
1 shallot, peeled
   and finely chopped
1 garlic clove,
   peeled and crushed
350g Arborio risotto rice
150ml dry white wine
sea salt

Put roughly two thirds of the mushrooms in a bowl, pour over the hot stock and leave to soak for 15 minutes. Strain the stock through a sieve into a saucepan, reserving the mushrooms, then set the pan over a low heat.

Meanwhile, put the remaining dried porcini in a spice grinder or small food processor and blend to a smooth powder. Combine the powder and Parmesan with 50g of the butter to make a smooth paste then spoon into a small bowl and chill.

Heat a splash of olive oil with the remaining butter in a shallow, heavy-based saucepan over a medium heat. Add the shallot and garlic and fry for 3 minutes until soft. Increase the temperature, add the soaked mushrooms and fry for 3–4 minutes. Add the rice and fry, stirring, for 1 minute until the grains start to turn translucent around the edges. Pour in the wine and bring to the boil, then leave to bubble away for a minute or so to burn off the alcohol. Add a ladleful of the hot stock and cook over a medium heat, stirring, until almost all the stock has been absorbed. Add the remaining stock gradually and continue to cook, stirring regularly, for about 10 minutes or until the rice is cooked but still retains a bit of bite. At this stage, the risotto should be slightly wetter than usual, but the porcini powder will soak up the excess liquid and adjust the texture once added.

Remove the pan from the heat, cover with a lid and leave to stand for 3–4 minutes. Beat in the chilled porcini butter mixture, season to taste with salt and serve.

Spinach and Ricotta Agnolotti

SERVES 4

These electric green little parcels, stuffed with ricotta and nutmeg, are as much fun to make as they are to eat. If you've never made pasta before, this dough is incredibly easy and very forgiving, and if you've never made filled pasta before, this is the perfect place to start. Rather than having to fill and shape each piece individually, as with tortellini or ravioli, you can fill entire strips of pasta and make a large batch in a fraction of the time. If you want to make the agnolotti ahead of time, leave them to dry at room temperature for 30 minutes, then keep them chilled until you're ready to cook.

fine polenta or semolina,
  for dusting
fine sea salt

FOR THE PASTA DOUGH:
250g '00' pasta flour,
  plus extra for dusting
150g baby leaf spinach,
  washed and patted dry
1 medium egg yolk
pinch of fine sea salt

FOR THE FILLING:
250g ricotta
30g Parmesan,
  finely grated,
  plus extra to serve
freshly grated nutmeg
freshly ground black
  pepper

TO SERVE:
50g cold butter, cubed
Brown Butter
  (page 205) or
  extra virgin olive oil

Put all the ingredients for the pasta dough in a food processor and blend until the mixture forms a smooth dough. Turn the dough out onto a clean work surface and knead for a couple of minutes until silky smooth, then wrap in clingfilm and chill in the fridge for 30 minutes.

Meanwhile, beat together the ingredients for the filling, season to taste with nutmeg and black pepper and spoon into a piping bag fitted with a 1cm plain nozzle.

Using a pasta machine, roll the dough out using the widest setting. Fold the dough in half, give it a quarter turn and roll it out again. Repeat this process three more times until the pasta is shiny and feels stronger. Cut the dough in half, then set the machine to the next thinnest setting and roll out into one long sheet. Keep rolling both sheets of pasta, working down through the settings each time you roll, until you reach the second-to-thinnest setting. Cover one sheet of pasta with clingfilm and set aside.

Lightly dust the work surface with a little flour and lay the sheet of pasta widthways. Pipe a 1cm-thick line of the filling along the edge nearest to you, ensuring that you keep it straight. Carefully roll the sheet of pasta away from you just until the filling is enclosed, then brush a little water along the line on the dough where the filling is enclosed so that it is sealed in.

CONTINUED OVERLEAF

Spinach and Ricotta Agnolotti continued

Working along the tube of filled pasta, pinch with your thumb and forefinger to divide into 2.5cm parcels. Press down with your fingertip between each parcel to seal. Using a pastry wheel, trim the long edge of unfilled dough (furthest away from you), leaving about 1cm between the parcels and the trimmed edge. Cut each parcel with a sharp knife to separate, or use a pastry wheel if you have one. Dust a tray with fine polenta or semolina and transfer the finished agnolotti to the tray. Repeat with the remaining pasta sheet and filling.

To cook the agnolotti, bring a large pan of salted water to the boil and have a separate shallow pan ready next to it. Drop the agnolotti into the boiling water and cook for 3–4 minutes. About 1 minute before the pasta is ready, pour a ladleful of the cooking water into the second pan and bring to a simmer. Gradually whisk in the cold cubed butter until emulsified and thickened. Drain the agnolotti, add to the butter sauce and toss to coat.

Divide the pasta between warmed serving bowls, drizzle over a little Brown Butter or extra virgin olive oil and sprinkle with grated Parmesan.

Singapore Noodles

We often refer to these as 'kitchen sink noodles' in that you throw an entire fridge full of ingredients into the wok and it always tastes delicious. That's not to say it's a dish without refinement though; the spicing, seasoning and sauce all have to be spot on to marry together the assorted ingredients. Like any good stir-fry you should approach it as a marathon followed by a sprint; take time preparing all of the ingredients first so that you can grab them in quick succession once you start cooking. Everything should have its own texture too; if the pan gets crowded the vegetables and noodles can stew and overcook easily, which is why I only tend to make this to serve two people.

8 dried shiitake
  mushrooms
125g dried rice
  vermicelli noodles
1 duck egg or 2 medium
  chicken eggs
2 teaspoons sesame oil
1 tablespoon light
  soy sauce
groundnut oil or
  vegetable oil
1 onion, peeled
  and sliced
2 garlic cloves,
  peeled and chopped

1 tablespoon grated
  (peeled) fresh ginger
2 red bird's-eye chillies,
  finely sliced
1 tablespoon
  curry powder
1 teaspoon
  smoked paprika
100g fine green beans,
  trimmed and cut
  into thirds
1 red pepper, deseeded
  and finely sliced
1 carrot, peeled and cut
  into fine matchsticks
150g shredded Hispi
  (pointed) cabbage
  or Savoy cabbage,
  finely shredded

FOR THE SAUCE:
2 tablespoons
  vegetarian oyster
  sauce
1 tablespoon dark
  soy sauce
1 tablespoon
  rice vinegar

TO SERVE:
2 spring onions,
  finely sliced
1 small bunch of
  coriander, chopped

Pour boiling water over the dried mushrooms and leave to soak for 30 minutes, then drain, reserving the water. Remove and discard the mushroom stalks and slice the caps. Set aside.

Soak the noodles in boiling water for 3 minutes, then drain and refresh under cold running water. Spread the noodles out on a large plate to stop them from clumping together.

Beat together the egg(s), sesame oil and soy sauce and set aside. Mix the ingredients for the sauce together and set aside.

Heat a splash of groundnut or vegetable oil in a wok over a high heat until smoking, add the onion, garlic, ginger and chillies and stir-fry for 2 minutes. Add the spices and stir-fry for 1 minute. Add a splash of the reserved mushroom water, then add all the prepared vegetables and stir-fry for a few minutes.

Push all the ingredients to one side of the wok, pour in the beaten egg mixture and leave to cook, undisturbed, for 1 minute until set, then roughly break it up with your spatula or spoon and toss through the vegetables.

Add the noodles and toss to combine, then pour over the sauce mixture and give everything a quick mix. If it feels a little dry at any point or if ingredients start to stick to the base of the wok, just add a splash more mushroom water.

Remove the wok from the heat, then divide the contents between two warmed bowls, scatter over the spring onions and coriander and serve.

Okonomiyaki

These Japanese pancakes are as fun to make as they are to say; the name literally translates as 'how you like it', which I take to mean that you can add pretty much any combination of ingredients. The most important thing is to slice all of the vegetables finely enough so that they cook at the same rate and retain a little crunch. It's possible to buy specific okonomiyaki flour in Japanese food shops, but a combination of plain flour and cornflour does the trick just as well.

150g plain flour
20g cornflour
300ml Vegetable Stock
  (page 200)
5 medium eggs
1 medium sweet potato,
  peeled and grated
1 large Hispi (pointed)
  cabbage, shredded
8 fresh shiitake
  mushrooms,
  thinly sliced
6 spring onions,
  finely sliced
80g shredded
  red pickled ginger
generous pinch
  of fine sea salt
groundnut oil, for frying

FOR THE SAUCE:
6 tablespoons
  tomato ketchup
2 tablespoons
  Mushroom Ketchup
  (page 204)
2 tablespoons dark
  soy sauce
1½ teaspoons dark
  brown soft sugar

TO SERVE:
Kewpie (Japanese)
  mayonnaise
aonori (seaweed flakes
  – optional)

Mix together the plain flour and cornflour in a large bowl and make a well in the centre. Whisk together the stock and eggs, pour into the well and gradually whisk into the flour mixture until you have a smooth batter. Fold in the prepared vegetables and ginger and season with the salt.

Whisk together the ingredients for the sauce in a separate bowl and set aside.

Heat a splash of groundnut oil in a non-stick frying pan over a medium heat and pour in the vegetable mixture. For the first minute, shake the pan around and keep the vegetables moving, then let everything settle. Fry for 4 minutes without moving the pan, then cover the pan with a large plate and flip over both the plate and pan together so that the pancake falls onto the plate. Add a little more oil to the pan, then slide the pancake back into the pan and cook for a further 4–5 minutes until the pancake is set and the vegetables are crisp around the edges.

Slide the pancake onto a warmed serving plate and brush the sauce over the top. Drizzle over the mayonnaise and top with the aonori, if using. Cut into wedges and serve.

Baingan Bharta

This is essentially an Indian version of that classic smoky aubergine dish, Baba Ghanoush. The aubergines need to be cooked until they're deeply charred all over and starting to collapse in on themselves. When they're cool enough to handle, split them open and you'll be rewarded with sweet, smoky flesh that can stand up to some pretty bold flavours. Try to get fresh curry leaves if you can; the way they crackle when they hit the pan and release their heady fragrance is something I'll never tire of.

2 large aubergines
1 tablespoon
  vegetable oil
1 teaspoon
  cumin seeds
1 large onion, peeled
  and finely chopped
2 green chillies,
  roughly chopped
3 garlic cloves,
  peeled and crushed
30g fresh ginger,
  peeled and grated
12 fresh curry leaves
½ teaspoon
  ground asafoetida
½ teaspoon
  ground turmeric
4 tomatoes, diced
1 teaspoon
  garam masala
juice of ½ lemon
1 small bunch
  of coriander,
  finely chopped
sea salt and
  freshly ground
  black pepper
warm parathas,
  to serve

Preheat the grill to a high heat and line a baking tray with foil. Pierce the aubergines with the tip of a knife to prevent them from bursting open as they cook, then lay them on the lined baking tray and grill for 25 minutes, turning occasionally – the skins should be black and crisp all over. Transfer them to a chopping board and leave them to sit until they're cool enough to handle.

Cut the aubergines in half lengthways and scoop out the flesh with a spoon, discarding any pieces of charred skin. Roughly chop the smoky flesh.

Heat the vegetable oil in a deep sauté pan over a medium heat, add the cumin seeds and fry for a minute. Add the onion and fry for about 10 minutes until soft and caramelised. Add the chillies, garlic and ginger and fry for a couple of minutes until softened. Then add the curry leaves, asafoetida and turmeric and fry for a minute, stirring. Stir in the tomatoes and simmer gently for 10 minutes until they have broken down. Add the aubergine flesh, stir in the garam masala and cook for a further couple of minutes.

Remove the pan from the heat and stir in the lemon juice and coriander. Season to taste with salt and black pepper and serve with warm parathas.

Lotus Leaf Parcels with Shiitake Mushrooms

MAKES 8

These delicious parcels are a meat-free version of one of my favourite dim sum dishes: *Lo Mai Gai*. They're traditionally steamed in dried lotus leaves which impart a tea-like fragrance as the rice steams. Lotus leaves are available in Chinese supermarkets or through online retailers, but if you can't find them a moistened sheet of greaseproof paper will work as a substitute. If you're planning on making a Chinese feast for the family, serve these alongside the Steam-fried Buns (page 51) and the Vegetable Wontons with Chilli Oil (page 110).

350g Chinese glutinous rice or Thai sticky rice
1 tablespoon dark soy sauce
½ teaspoon ground white pepper
4 dried lotus leaves
vegetable oil
250g fresh shiitake mushrooms, stalks discarded and caps chopped
1 bunch of spring onions, chopped
2 garlic cloves, peeled and chopped
30g fresh ginger, peeled and grated
3 tablespoons unsalted roasted peanuts, chopped
pinch of Chinese five-spice powder
2 tablespoons vegetarian oyster sauce
2 tablespoons Shaoxing rice wine or dry sherry
1 tablespoon light soy sauce
2 teaspoons cornflour

Soak the rice in cold water for 2 hours, then drain thoroughly. Mix with the soy sauce and white pepper, then set aside. Meanwhile, soak the lotus leaves in warm water for 1 hour.

Heat a splash of vegetable oil in a wok or large frying pan over a high heat, add half the mushrooms and stir-fry for 5 minutes until browned. Remove from the pan and repeat with the remaining mushrooms. Heat a little more oil in the pan and stir-fry the spring onions, garlic and ginger over a high heat for 2–3 minutes until softened. Add the peanuts and stir-fry for 1 minute. Return the mushrooms to the pan with all the remaining ingredients and cook, stirring, for 1 minute until the mixture has thickened slightly, then remove the pan from the heat and stir in the rice. Leave to cool for a few minutes.

While the rice mixture is cooling, drain the lotus leaves, then cut away the thick central stalks to leave you with eight pieces of leaf. Lay the leaves out on a large board, then divide the cooled rice mixture equally between them. Wrap each up into a neat parcel, then lay them, seam-side down, in a bamboo steamer; if they look like they might unravel, you can secure the parcels with kitchen string. Steam for 1 hour 20 minutes, then unwrap at the table and serve hot.

Fennel Tarte Fine

SERVES 6

This is my savoury version of the classic French *Tarte Fine Aux Pommes*, a wafer thin, buttery apple tart which is a dish of real beauty. The trick is weighing down the tart as it bakes; this gives a crisp base and, perhaps more importantly, stops the pastry from rising too high and knocking the toppings off.

2 small fennel bulbs
plain flour, for dusting
320g block of all-butter
    puff pastry
75g mascarpone
sea salt and freshly
    ground black pepper
olive oil, for brushing
1 teaspoon icing sugar
1 medium egg yolk
1 tablespoon whole milk
2 tablespoons finely
    grated pecorino

Preheat the oven to 180°C/gas mark 4. Trim the leafy green fronds from the tops of the fennel, drop into a small bowl of cold water and chill in the fridge. Put the fennel bulbs in a saucepan, pour over enough boiling water to cover and bring to the boil. Reduce the heat slightly and leave to simmer for 10 minutes. Drain off the water, then leave to finish draining and to cool on kitchen paper.

Meanwhile, lightly dust a work surface with flour and roll out the pastry to the thickness of about 3mm. Using a dinner plate or the base of a cake tin, cut out a round roughly 24cm in diameter. Line a baking tray with greaseproof paper, then slide the pastry round onto the lined tray. Prick all over with a fork, leaving a 2cm border clear around the edge. Season the mascarpone with a pinch of salt and plenty of black pepper then spread over the pastry in an even layer, leaving the border around the edge clear. Put the baking tray in the freezer for 10 minutes to firm the pastry.

Thinly slice the fennel and blot any excess moisture with a few sheets of kitchen paper. Arrange the fennel slices over the mascarpone mixture on the pastry, then brush with a light film of olive oil. Dust the fennel with the icing sugar and season with a little salt. Mix together the egg yolk and milk, then brush the mixture around the edge of the pastry.

Lay a sheet of greaseproof paper on top of the tart and top with a thin baking tray. Bake for 20 minutes, then remove the top tray and greaseproof paper. Scatter over the pecorino and bake for a further 10 minutes until the fennel is golden brown and the pastry is crisp. Slide the tart onto a board and serve.

Pumpkin Risotto

SERVES 4

I hate wasting food so this recipe makes me very happy as it uses every last scrap of the pumpkin; roasted, puréed and as flavouring for the stock (and a good stock is pivotal when making risotto). I make this year-round with butternut squash, but the flavour and colour is even better towards the end of summer when the early autumn varieties of pumpkin start to make an appearance. I love to finish this risotto with crispy fried sage leaves – the perfect partner for sweet pumpkin – but if you'd rather not dirty another pan, you can finely chop the leaves and stir through the risotto just before serving.

1 small pumpkin
  (about 800g) or
  butternut squash,
  peeled and deseeded
olive oil
1 litre hot Pumpkin Stock
  (page 200)
20g butter
1 shallot, peeled
  and finely chopped
1 garlic clove,
  peeled and crushed
pinch of freshly
  grated nutmeg
350g Arborio risotto rice
150ml dry vermouth
  or dry white wine

TO FINISH THE RISOTTO:

25g cold butter,
  cubed
50g Parmesan,
  finely grated
12 sage leaves
pinch of sea salt

Preheat the oven to 180°C/gas mark 4. Line a roasting tray with greaseproof paper. Dice half the pumpkin into 1cm cubes, toss in a little olive oil and tip into the lined roasting tray. Roast for 20–25 minutes until soft and caramelised. Remove from the oven and set aside.

Meanwhile, coarsely grate the remaining pumpkin, put in a saucepan and pour in 250ml of the hot stock. Bring to the boil, then reduce the heat and simmer for 10 minutes until the pumpkin is soft. Pour the contents of the pan into a liquidiser and blend until smooth, then set aside.

Heat a splash of olive oil with the butter in a shallow, heavy-based saucepan over a medium heat, add the shallot and garlic and fry for 3 minutes until soft. Stir in the nutmeg and rice and fry for a minute, stirring constantly. Pour in the vermouth or wine, bring to the boil and let it bubble away for a minute or so to burn off the alcohol. Add a ladleful of the remaining hot stock and cook, stirring, over a medium heat until almost all of it has been absorbed. Gradually add the remaining stock in the same way, continuing to cook the risotto for about 10 minutes or until the rice is cooked but still retains a bit of bite.

Remove the pan from the heat, cover with a lid and leave to stand for 3–4 minutes. Beat in the cold butter and Parmesan, fold through the pumpkin purée and leave to stand while you fry the sage leaves.

Heat a generous glug of olive oil in a frying pan over a medium-high heat, add the sage leaves and fry for 30–40 seconds until crisp. Drain on kitchen paper and season with the salt.

Divide the risotto between four warmed serving bowls and spoon the roasted pumpkin over the rice. Crumble the fried sage leaves over the top and serve.

Caramelised Onion Soup with Cheddar

SERVES 4

The key to this recipe is patience; the onions need to cook slowly and gently until they turn a deep chestnut brown and become rich, sticky and sweet. I make this in an old cast-iron casserole and as the onions cook a sort of sweet lacquer starts to coat the inside of the pan, adding loads of flavour to the finished soup. I finish it with crispy baked Cheddar, the sort of stuff you get when making cheese on toast and a little cheese drops onto the grill tray and turns really crispy. Delicious.

50g unsalted butter
5 onions,
  peeled and thinly sliced
1 fresh bay leaf
150g vintage Cheddar,
  grated
2 sprigs of thyme,
  leaves picked, plus
  extra leaves to serve
1 teaspoon light brown
  soft sugar
400ml dry cider
400ml Vegetable Stock
  (page 200)
200ml double cream
sea salt and
  white pepper

Melt the butter in a large, heavy-based pan over a low heat, add the onions and bay leaf and fry very gently for 35–40 minutes until sticky and caramelised, stirring occasionally. The onions should be a deep brown colour, but take care that they don't catch, as you'll lose their wonderful sweetness.

Meanwhile, preheat the oven to 160°C/gas mark 3. Line a baking tray with greaseproof paper, scatter over the grated cheese in an even layer and bake for 15–20 minutes until melted and crisp. Remove from the oven, blot the oil from the cheese with kitchen paper and leave to cool.

Increase the heat under the onions slightly, add the thyme and sugar and cook for a couple of minutes until the sugar has melted. Pour in the cider and bring to the boil, then reduce the heat and simmer until reduced by half. Pour in the stock and cream, return to a simmer and cook gently for 20 minutes. Remove the bay leaf, pour the mixture into a liquidiser and blend until smooth.

Pour the soup into warmed serving bowls and crumble the baked cheese over the top. Finish with a scattering of thyme leaves and serve.

The Best Truffle Pasta

SERVES 4

This is less of a recipe and more of a way to serve one of my favourite ingredients. Truffles hold a certain mystique; those who hunt them keep their locations a safely guarded secret and as a result they're regarded as an expensive luxury. However, they're at their best when served as simply as possible, so the overall cost of the dish isn't actually that high. With truffles, everything is about aroma, so they need to be as fresh as possible. So called 'truffle-infused' oils aren't really a worthy substitute; they taste of chemicals and certainly don't have the same wow factor. This is a dish for a special occasion.

fine sea salt
400g dried tagliatelle,
    tonnarelli or spaghetti
1 large, fresh
    black truffle
100g cold unsalted
    butter, cubed
75g Parmesan,
    finely grated

Bring a large pan of water to the boil and salt it generously. Add the pasta and cook for 2 minutes less than the packet instructions. Meanwhile, finely dice half the truffle.

Just before the pasta is ready, set a wide sauté pan over a medium heat and add a ladleful of the pasta water. Let it bubble and reduce for a minute, then gradually whisk in the cold butter and diced truffle until emulsified. Remove the pan from the heat and gradually whisk in the Parmesan and a little more pasta water until you have a smooth, silky sauce.

Drain the pasta and give it a thorough shake in the colander; this will dry the pasta and cool it slightly so that the sauce doesn't overheat and split. Tip the pasta into the sauce and use a pair of tongs to toss and turn the pasta until the strands are evenly coated with the sauce.

Divide between warmed serving bowls, then shave or grate the remaining truffle over the top at the table.

Gnudi with Tomato Sauce

SERVES 4

These light ricotta dumplings (pronounced 'noo-di') are just that, a sort of naked ravioli; all filling and no pasta shell. The secret lies in burying balls of ricotta and Parmesan in semolina and chilling overnight. The semolina draws the moisture from the cheese and forms a fine skin around the outside so that they keep their shape when cooked. I've had these in various forms; some mixed with spinach, others served with brown butter and sage. However, the combination of pillowy-light-but-rich cheese dumplings and an intense, garlicky tomato sauce is hard to beat.

FOR THE GNUDI:
1kg fine semolina,
  plus extra for dusting
500g ricotta
60g Parmesan,
  finely grated, plus
  extra to serve
fine sea salt

FOR THE SAUCE:
800g San Marzano
  tomatoes or ripe
  plum tomatoes,
  roughly chopped
3 tablespoons extra
  virgin olive oil
3 garlic cloves, peeled
  and wafer thinly sliced
pinch of sugar
4 sprigs of oregano,
  leaves picked
sea salt and freshly
  ground black pepper

The day before you plan to cook, make the *gnudi*. Cover a large roasting tray with one third of the semolina. Beat the ricotta and Parmesan together until smooth. Now have a taste and add a pinch of fine sea salt if you feel it needs it.

Spoon the mixture into a piping bag fitted with a 2.5cm plain nozzle. Pipe lengths of the mixture onto a work surface dusted with a little semolina, then cut the ricotta 'sausages' into 2.5cm lengths. Roll each piece into a ball, laying them in the prepared tray as you go, ensuring that the *gnudi* don't touch. Keep working until all the ricotta mixture has been rolled, then gently scatter the remaining semolina over the dumplings until they're completely covered. Put the tray, uncovered, into the fridge and leave to chill overnight.

The next day, start by making the sauce. Pulse the tomatoes in a food processor to a semi-smooth purée. Pour the oil into a cold sauté pan, add the garlic and set over a low heat. Cook gently for 5 minutes or until the garlic just starts to turn golden around the edges, then immediately add the tomatoes, sugar and oregano. Bring to a simmer and cook for 10–15 minutes until thickened. Season to taste with salt and black pepper.

Meanwhile, bring a large pan of salted water to the boil. Fish the *gnudi* out of the semolina and into a colander, then shake off any excess semolina. Add to the pan in one go and cook for 2–3 minutes or until they float to the surface. Working quickly, use a large skimmer or slotted spoon to transfer the *gnudi* straight into the pan of tomato sauce. Add a splash of the cooking water to the sauce and gently toss the *gnudi* to coat in the sauce.

Divide the *gnudi* between warmed serving bowls and top with a little grated Parmesan.

Sichuan-spiced Aubergine

SERVES 4

Also known as 'fish-fragrant aubergine', this dish is all about the deep, rich sauce layered with flavour. Sichuan peppercorns add a delightfully addictive tongue-numbing heat; just make sure that you don't fry them for too long with the chillies or they will make the sauce turn bitter.

3 aubergines
groundnut oil
4 dried red chillies,
   crumbled
2 teaspoons
   Sichuan peppercorns,
   crushed
4 garlic cloves, peeled
   and finely chopped
30g fresh ginger,
   peeled and grated
6 spring onions,
   white parts finely
   chopped, green parts
   finely sliced

FOR THE SAUCE:
2 tablespoons
   chilli bean paste
2 tablespoons dark
   soy sauce
2 tablespoons
   Chinkiang black rice
   vinegar or good-
   quality balsamic
   vinegar
2 tablespoons Shaoxing
   rice wine or dry sherry
2 teaspoons cornflour
1 teaspoon caster sugar

steamed jasmine rice,
   to serve

Slice the aubergines into thirds widthways, then cut each section into six wedges. Heat a splash of groundnut oil in a wok over a high heat until smoking, add one third of the aubergine pieces and stir-fry for 5 minutes until golden brown and starting to soften. Tip onto a plate lined with kitchen paper to drain, then repeat with the remaining aubergine pieces.

Meanwhile, whisk together the ingredients for the sauce in a small bowl and set aside.

Heat a little more oil in the wok, add the chillies and peppercorns and fry for a few seconds until they start to darken. Immediately add the garlic, ginger and spring onion whites and stir-fry for a couple of minutes. Add the sauce mixture to the wok and let everything bubble up for a minute or so, then slide the aubergines into the sauce. Stir gently to coat, then let everything simmer gently for 2–3 minutes; if the mixture looks a little dry, add a splash of hot water.

Tip into a warmed serving dish and scatter over the reserved spring onion greens. Serve with steamed jasmine rice.

Fresh Corn Tamales

MAKES 12

Tamales are usually made only with masa harina, a type of fine Mexican cornmeal similar to polenta, and wrapped in rehydrated dried corn husks. However, when sweetcorn is available in abundance during the summer months, I prefer to make them with fresh corn and steam them in their vibrant green outer leaves.

4 corn on the cob
  in their husks
olive oil
1 bunch of spring onions,
  chopped
½ teaspoon chipotle
  chilli flakes
150g butter, softened
1 tablespoon
  caster sugar
1 teaspoon
  baking powder
1 teaspoon sea salt
150g masa harina,
  plus a little extra
  if needed
200g feta, crumbled
Mexican chilli sauce,
  to serve

Bring a large pan of water to the boil. Strip the leaves from the corn, taking care not to tear them as you go. Discard any of the silky fibres, then drop the leaves into the boiling water and blanch for 1 minute. Drain and pat dry.

Heat a little olive oil in a frying pan, add the spring onions and chilli flakes and fry for 2–3 minutes until soft. Remove the pan from the heat and leave to cool.

Using a serrated knife, slice the kernels from the corn cobs, then tip into a food processor and blend to a smooth purée. Transfer to a large bowl, add the spring onion mixture, butter, sugar, baking powder and salt and mix together until combined. Then gradually mix in enough masa harina to form a thick batter. Fold in the crumbled feta.

Divide the mixture between the 12 largest corn leaves. Wrap each into a neat parcel, then lay, seam-side down, in a steamer. Steam the tamales for 1¼ hours until cooked through, then unwrap at the table and serve hot with Mexican chilli sauce.

Vegetable Wontons with Chilli Oil

SERVES 4

A steaming bowlful of these wontons is the perfect pick-me-up; slippery, juicy and dressed with an addictively spicy chilli oil. This recipe is one of my ultimate hangover cures, reheated or even eaten straight from the fridge. Don't judge me.

vegetable oil
2 garlic cloves, peeled
   and finely chopped
30g fresh ginger, peeled
   and finely chopped
4 spring onions,
   white parts finely
   chopped, green
   parts sliced
1 carrot, peeled
   and finely chopped
200g rainbow chard,
   stalks finely chopped
   and leaves shredded
1 teaspoon cornflour
   mixed with
   2 tablespoons
   vegetarian oyster
   sauce until smooth
light soy sauce, to taste
32 wonton wrappers
1.5 litres Vegetable Stock
   (page 200)

TO SERVE:
4 tablespoons
   Chinese roast chilli oil
1 tablespoon
   Chinkiang black rice
   vinegar or rice vinegar
1 teaspoon toasted
   sesame oil

Heat a little vegetable oil in a wok over a high heat, add the garlic, ginger and spring onion whites and stir-fry for a couple of minutes until softened. Then add the carrot and stir-fry for 2–3 minutes until softened. Next add the chard stalks and stir-fry for a couple of minutes, then add the chard leaves and stir-fry for 1 minute until the leaves start to wilt. Stir in the cornflour and oyster sauce mixture, season to taste with light soy sauce and cook briefly, stirring, until thickened. Remove from the heat and leave to cool.

Meanwhile, combine the chilli oil, vinegar and sesame oil in a small saucepan and bring to a gentle simmer, then remove from the heat.

Line a baking tray with greaseproof paper. To form the dumplings, take a small spoonful of the vegetable mixture and place in the centre of a wonton wrapper. Lightly moisten one edge with a little water, then fold one tip of the wrapper over to meet the opposite tip to form a triangle. Press the edges together to seal. Working along the longest edge, wrap the opposite corners around your little finger to meet, then pinch together to seal. Transfer to the lined tray. Repeat with the remaining wrappers and filling.

Bring the stock to the boil in a pan. Add the wontons, in batches, to the stock and cook for 2–3 minutes. Remove with a slotted spoon and divide between warmed serving bowls, then spoon over a little of the hot stock — you don't need much, just enough to moisten the wontons.

Reheat the chilli oil mixture, spoon over the wontons and scatter over the spring onion greens to serve.

Indian Stuffed Potatoes

SERVES 4

If I were to become a full-time vegetarian, then Indian food, and in particular that of northern India, would be my cuisine of choice. The first time we visited India, we only realised after about a week that we hadn't eaten any meat; their vegetarian cuisine is so varied and so delicious that we hadn't missed it one bit. Traditionally this Kashmiri dish is made with small potatoes, but I find larger ones far less fiddly to prepare.

1 tablespoon ghee
  or vegetable oil
2 medium onions,
  peeled and finely sliced
4 garlic cloves,
  peeled and crushed
40g fresh ginger,
  peeled and grated
2 green chillies,
  finely chopped
2 teaspoons
  garam masala
1 teaspoon
  ground cumin
1 teaspoon
  ground turmeric
1 teaspoon
  kashmiri chilli powder
4 tomatoes, diced
2 tablespoons
  ground almonds
250ml water
sea salt
4 large Charlotte potatoes
vegetable oil,
  for deep-frying

FOR THE STUFFING:
200g paneer, grated
1 teaspoon
  fennel seeds, crushed
1 teaspoon
  cumin seeds, crushed
½ teaspoon kashmiri
  chilli powder
½ teaspoon
  ground coriander

chopped coriander,
  to serve

First make the sauce. Heat the ghee or oil in a saucepan, add the onions and cook gently for 10 minutes until softened and caramelised. Add the garlic and ginger and fry, stirring, for 2–3 minutes, then add the chillies and ground spices and fry, continuing to stir, for 1 minute. Stir in the tomatoes and cook over a high heat for 5 minutes until they start to break down. Add the ground almonds and pour in the water, then bring to a simmer and cook for 15 minutes. Season to taste with salt, then remove the pan from the heat and leave to cool slightly. Pour the mixture into a liquidiser and blend until smooth.

Peel the potatoes and trim the ends so that they stand upright on a flat surface. Using a melon baller, hollow out the potatoes to leave a shell about 5mm thick; the scooped-out potato flesh is not needed for the recipe, but it's worth keeping for mash or soups.

Heat the vegetable oil for deep-frying in a large saucepan to 180°C. Add the potato shells and fry, turning occasionally, for 5 minutes until golden brown; the potatoes aren't meant to be fully cooked at this point, so don't worry if they still seem firm. Remove from the oil with a slotted spoon and drain on kitchen paper.

Mix together the ingredients for the stuffing in a small bowl and season with a pinch of salt. Divide the stuffing between the potato shells, taking care not to break them. Pour half the sauce into a saucepan just big enough to hold the potatoes. Sit the stuffed potatoes on top, then pour the remaining sauce around them. Bring to a gentle simmer, then cover the pan and cook for 10 minutes. Uncover the pan and cook for a further 5 minutes, basting the tops of the potatoes regularly with the sauce. Remove the pan from the heat and leave to stand for 5 minutes to allow the potatoes to soak up more of the sauce. Serve scattered with chopped coriander.

Celeriac and Kale Pithivier

SERVES 6

A pithivier is essentially a free-form puff pastry pie that can be filled with virtually anything. This recipe uses two of my favourite autumnal ingredients: earthy celeriac and iron-rich leafy kale. Make sure that the filling isn't too wet and bake the pie on a preheated pizza stone or heavy baking tray to avoid the dreaded soggy bottom.

plain flour, for dusting
500g block of
  all-butter puff pastry
fine sea salt
1 celeriac
  (about 900g–1kg),
  peeled and cut into
  3mm slices
300g kale or cavolo nero
  (black kale), stalks
  removed (see page
  133), leaves shredded
150ml double cream
2 garlic cloves,
  peeled and crushed
pinch of freshly
  grated nutmeg
sea salt and
  freshly ground
  black pepper
2 medium eggs,
  beaten

Dust the work surface with flour, then roll out the pastry into a large rectangle 3mm thick. Use a large dinner plate to cut out two circles of pastry roughly 25cm in diameter. Sandwich a piece of greaseproof paper between them, then slide them onto a baking tray and chill for 30 minutes.

Bring a large pan of salted water to the boil. Drop the celeriac into the boiling water and simmer for 5 minutes. Remove from the pan with a slotted spoon and set aside to cool. Add the kale to the pan and blanch for 1 minute, then drain and refresh under cold running water. Pat dry with kitchen paper, then finely chop.

Meanwhile, bring the cream, garlic and nutmeg to the boil in a small saucepan, then reduce the heat and simmer for 5 minutes. Mix together the celeriac, kale and cream mixture in a bowl and season to taste with salt and black pepper, then leave to cool.

Line a baking tray with greaseproof paper and lay one of the pastry circles on top. Brush a 2cm border of beaten egg around the outside of the pastry, then pile the filling into the middle. Lay the second pastry circle on top and press down around the edges to seal. Brush the pastry with the beaten egg and chill for 15 minutes. Brush with a second coat of beaten egg and chill again.

Preheat the oven to 190°C/gas mark 5 and put a pizza stone or heavy baking tray in the oven. Remove the pithivier from the fridge and trim around the edge to neaten, then use a small, round pastry cutter to cut a hole in the middle of the pastry lid to let the steam escape. Using a small, sharp knife, score evenly spaced curved lines down from the top of the pithivier. Using the greaseproof paper, slide the pithivier onto the heated pizza stone or baking tray and bake for 35 minutes until golden brown. If the pastry starts to get a little dark, cover it loosely with foil for the final 10 minutes. Remove from the oven and leave to stand for 10–15 minutes before serving.

Winter Vegetable Frittata

This recipe is a great way of using up odd bits of vegetables; I always have eggs in the house so any fridge raiding tends to turn into some sort of omelette or frittata. Make sure that the vegetables are just cooked through and well seasoned before adding the eggs, as once they hit the pan there's no going back. Keep an eye on the wobble too – the eggs should be very lightly set rather than completely firm.

2 carrots
1 parsnip
½ small celeriac
   (about 350g)
olive oil
30g butter
2 garlic cloves,
   peeled and crushed
2 sprigs of thyme,
   leaves picked
a large handful of kale
   or sprout tops,
   kale stalks removed
   (see page 133),
   leaves shredded
8 medium eggs,
   beaten
150g Stilton or
   goat's cheese,
   crumbled

Preheat the grill to a medium–high heat. Peel the carrots, parsnip and celeriac, then cut into long, thin matchsticks.

Heat a splash of olive oil in a large, non–stick frying pan over a medium–high heat. Add the butter and once it's foaming, add the vegetable matchsticks and fry for 5–6 minutes until softened, stirring regularly. Add the garlic and thyme and fry, stirring, for a couple of minutes, then increase the heat, add the greens and fry for 2–3 minutes until softened. Remove the pan from the heat.

Ensure that the vegetables are evenly distributed over the base of the pan, then pour over the beaten eggs. Sprinkle the cheese over the top, then return the pan to the hob over a very low heat. Cook the eggs just enough to set the underside, then slide the pan under the grill (protect the handle from the heat if it isn't heatproof) and cook for a few minutes until the eggs are lightly set with a gentle wobble in the middle of the pan. Remove the pan from the grill and leave to stand for 2–3 minutes before turning out and slicing. Serve either hot or at room temperature.

SIDES

White Beans with Nettles and Pesto

SERVES 2
AS A SIDE
OR SERVES 4
AS A MAIN

If you've never cooked with nettles before, now's the time to give it a go. They're delicious, readily available and, most importantly, won't cost you a penny. The sting is neutralised during cooking so you're left with bright green leaves with a flavour somewhere between spinach and cucumber. Wild nettles need to be harvested before they flower, so choose younger plants with smaller leaves, and, as with any foraging, only pick plants if you're certain of their identity. Make sure that you wear a sturdy pair of gloves and wash the nettles thoroughly to get rid of any dust or insects.

2 tablespoons extra
   virgin olive oil
2 plum tomatoes,
   deseeded and diced
1 garlic clove, peeled
   and crushed
600g jar Spanish
   haricot beans
300ml Vegetable Stock
   (page 200)
200g wild nettle leaves,
   washed

FOR THE PESTO:
75ml light olive oil
50g pine nuts
1 small garlic clove,
   peeled
25g Parmesan,
   finely grated
pinch of sea salt
80g basil leaves

chargrilled sourdough
   bread drizzled with
   peppery olive oil,
   to serve

Heat the extra virgin olive oil in a saucepan over a medium heat, add the tomatoes and garlic and fry gently for 5 minutes until softened. Add the beans with their liquid from the jar and stir to combine. Pour over the stock, bring to a simmer and cook gently for 5 minutes.

Meanwhile, put all the ingredients for the pesto, except the basil leaves, in a food processor and blend until smooth. Add the basil and blend again to a smooth paste.

Stir the nettle leaves into the bean mixture and cook for a further minute, then remove from the heat. Divide between warmed serving bowls and top each portion with a spoonful of the pesto. Serve with chargrilled sourdough drizzled with peppery olive oil.

Green Beans with Kimchi Butter

SERVES 4

This recipe is all about the kimchi butter. I originally made it to serve with roast chicken, but then found it worked beautifully with simple green vegetables. Green beans with chilli and garlic is a classic combination, so this just takes it up a notch by adding the funk of kimchi and the deep roast chilli flavour of gochujang. This makes more kimchi butter than you need for this recipe, but it's not really worth making in smaller quantities. It keeps for a few weeks in the fridge and is a great way of jazzing up vegetables, potatoes or simple roast meat or fish.

200g kimchi
1 tablespoon gochujang
  (Korean hot red
  chilli paste)
200g unsalted butter,
  softened
fine sea salt
500g fine green beans,
  trimmed

Put the kimchi and gochujang in a liquidiser and blend until completely smooth. Scrape the paste onto a square of muslin cloth, then gather up the edges and give it a good squeeze to remove as much liquid as possible. Tie the loose edges together with string to make a neat parcel, then hang over a bowl or jug at room temperature for an hour to drain. You don't need the drained-off liquid for this recipe, but it's worth keeping for use in dressings or stir-fried dishes; pour it into a jar and keep in the fridge for up to a month.

Put the butter in a large bowl and whisk lightly. Gradually beat in the kimchi paste until smooth, then spoon onto a sheet of clingfilm. Roll up in the clingfilm into a sausage shape and twist the clingfilm at either end to seal. Chill in the fridge for 30 minutes until firm.

Bring a large pan of lightly salted water to the boil, add the green beans and cook for 4 minutes. Drain the beans and tip into a large bowl. Dice roughly one third of the kimchi butter, add to the bowl and toss until nearly all the butter has melted and coated the beans. Tip into a large serving dish and serve.

Smoky Potato Terrine

It may seem a little odd to use smoky bacon flavoured crisps in what is a fairly refined side dish, but they're there for good reason. As well as adding a sweet, smoky flavour, their inclusion increases the starch content and helps to bind the terrine together as it cools. I had to do a lot of research into all sorts of crisps when testing this recipe (tough job, you're welcome) and found that the majority are bacon-flavoured and don't contain any real bacon or pork products at all. If you really want to avoid them though, you can use a mixture of potato flour and sweet smoked paprika instead.

75g smoky bacon-
   flavoured crisps
1.5kg large Charlotte
   potatoes
100g butter, melted
sea salt

Preheat the oven to 180°C/gas mark 4. Put the crisps in a food processor and blend to a fine powder, then set aside. Peel the potatoes, square off the edges and thinly slice using a mandolin. Toss the potato slices in the melted butter, then arrange a layer of them in the bottom of a 900g loaf tin. After you've completed the layer, dust with a generous pinch of the powdered crisps and a pinch of salt. Continue layering and seasoning until all the potatoes have been used up, then cover the tin with foil and bake for 1½ hours; a small, sharp knife should slide into the potatoes with ease once they're ready.

Sit a second loaf tin on top of the potatoes and put a couple of heavy cans of food on top to weigh it down. Leave to cool, then chill in the fridgefor 3 hours or overnight if possible.

Turn the terrine out onto a chopping board and trim the edges to neaten, then cut into thick slices. Heat a dry non-stick frying pan over a medium heat and gently fry the slices for 2–3 minutes on each side until golden and crisp, then serve.

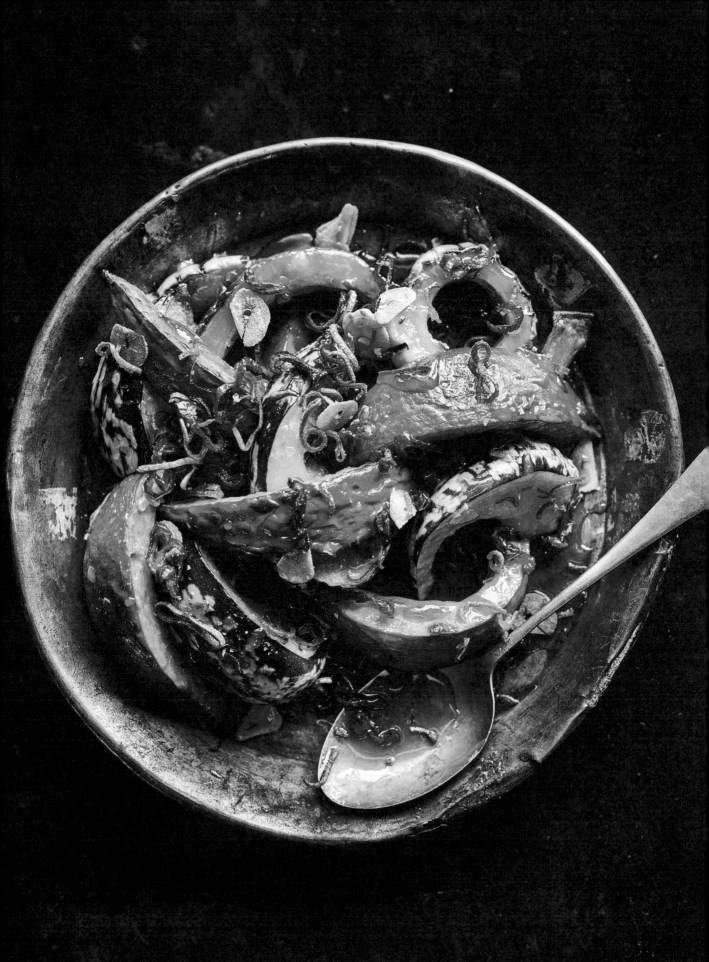

Miso-glazed Pumpkin

SERVES 4–6

As summer draws to a close, my local greengrocers' shelves start to fill with a jumble of autumnal pumpkins and squashes, from deep blue to electric orange and brilliant white ones. They roast beautifully and all but the very thick-skinned varieties can be cooked without needing to be peeled. The crunchy fried chillies, shallots and garlic need to be cooked very slowly, starting with the oil completely cold. They'll slowly expel any moisture and will eventually become glass-brittle, so make a perfect topping for the soft, sweet roast pumpkin.

2 small pumpkins,
 squash or a
 combination of both,
 deseeded and cut
 into thick wedges
olive oil
sea salt

FOR THE GLAZE:
6 tablespoons
 rice vinegar
4 tablespoons honey
4 tablespoons
 white miso paste
4 tablespoons mirin
1 teaspoon sesame oil

TO SERVE:
3 red chillies,
 finely sliced
2 shallots, peeled
 and finely sliced
350ml vegetable oil
4 garlic cloves,
 peeled and sliced

Preheat the oven to 220°C/gas mark 7. Put the pumpkin or squash wedges in a large bowl, drizzle with plenty of olive oil and toss to coat. Arrange in a single layer in a large roasting tray and season with salt. Roast for 30 minutes until soft and caramelised, turning halfway through.

Meanwhile, combine all the ingredients for the glaze in a small saucepan, bring to the boil and cook for 3–4 minutes until glossy and slightly thickened.

Put the chillies and shallots in a saucepan and pour over the vegetable oil. Gradually bring up to a medium heat and fry gently for 5 minutes until the shallots start to turn a golden colour at the edges. Add the garlic and fry for a further 5 minutes until the garlic and shallots are golden all over, stirring regularly. Immediately drain through a sieve (keep the oil for stir-fries) and tip onto a plate lined with kitchen paper. Season with a little salt while hot.

Arrange the pumpkin or squash wedges on a large serving platter and drizzle over the glaze, ensuring that everything gets a good coating. Scatter over the crispy chillies, shallots and garlic and serve.

IMAGE SHOWN ON PREVIOUS PAGE

Roast Carrots with Miso Honey Butter

SERVES 4

Sweet and salty flavours pair perfectly; think salted caramel or chocolate with a pinch of flaky sea salt. Simple roasted carrots are delicious in their own right, but when you dress them up with umami-rich miso paste and sweet, floral honey, it takes them to another level entirely. This has become a staple in our house to serve alongside roast chicken or pork, but as the flavours are subtle it goes with just about anything.

olive oil
6 medium carrots,
  scrubbed and halved
  lengthways
75g unsalted butter,
  softened
3 tablespoons
  white miso paste
2 tablespoons
  honey

Preheat the oven to 200°C/gas mark 6. Heat a thin layer of olive oil in a large frying over a medium heat, then add the carrots, cut-side down, and cook for 5 minutes, giving the pan a gentle shake occasionally. Beat the butter, miso paste and honey together, then add half to the pan; cover and chill the remaining butter mixture in the fridge. Continue to cook the carrots for a further 5 minutes, turning and basting them in the butter mixture.

Tip the carrots and butter mixture into a roasting tin (set the frying pan aside, uncleaned) and roast for 10–12 minutes until the carrots are tender but still retain a bit of bite. Remove from the oven and drain the carrots on kitchen paper.

Return the frying pan to the hob over a high heat and carefully lay in the carrots. Add the chilled butter mixture and cook, basting, for 2–3 minutes until the carrots are caramelised and sticky. Using a spatula, transfer to a warmed plate and serve.

IMAGE SHOWN ON FOLLOWING PAGE

Butter-roast Beetroot

SERVES 4–6

Juicy, vibrant and versatile, beetroot is well worth getting stained fingers for. Pickled beetroot has always been a favourite of mine; the earthy crunch works beautifully with sweet, sharp vinegar. This is essentially a warm version, albeit tempered by plenty of butter. It makes a great side dish to roast game or beef, but is easily transferred into a main course with the addition of some cooked lentils, crispy chicory and crumbled feta.

500g golf ball-sized
  beetroot (about 8–10),
  scrubbed and trimmed
120g butter
50ml sherry vinegar
4 sprigs of thyme
sea salt and freshly
  ground black pepper
150ml beetroot juice

Preheat the oven to 180°C/gas mark 4. Lay out a large sheet of foil, fold it in half lengthways and then fold in two of the open edges to make a bag. Combine the beetroot, 100g of the butter, the vinegar, thyme and salt and black pepper to taste in the bag, then seal the remaining open edge to make a parcel. Lay the parcel on a baking tray and roast for 1 hour until the beetroot is tender.

Meanwhile, bring the beetroot juice to the boil in a saucepan, then reduce the heat and simmer until reduced by half. Whisk in the remaining 20g butter and set aside.

Remove the beetroot from the parcel and, wearing gloves, carefully rub away the skins. Slice the beetroot in half, add to the pan and gently toss in the reduced juice. Pour into a warmed bowl and serve.

Glazed Turnips

SERVES 4

Turnips are robust, crunchy and peppery and are delicious roasted whole or braised and glazed. If you manage to find baby turnips with plenty of large, green leaves, you can flash-fry them in a separate pan then toss them with the glazed turnips just before serving.

2 bunches of
  baby turnips,
  approx. 500g
30g butter
100ml apple juice
100ml dry cider
2 sprigs of thyme
pinch of sea salt

Trim the roots and stems from the turnips, leaving a short length of stalk on each. If any are particularly large, slice them in half lengthways.

Put the turnips in a saucepan with all the remaining ingredients, except the salt, and bring to a simmer. Cook for 15 minutes, stirring occasionally, until almost all the liquid has been absorbed.

Remove the thyme, then increase the heat and cook for 5 minutes until the turnips are golden and glazed, shaking the pan regularly. Season with the salt and serve.

Leeks Vinaigrette with Cured Egg Yolk

SERVES 4

Poireau à la vinaigrette is about as old-school French classic as it gets and, as with all the best dishes, is wonderfully simple. For some reason though, bistros in France always seem to serve it chilled, totally killing the flavour. I think it works best just above room temperature so that the warmth of the leeks brings out the flavour of the vinaigrette. My version is finished with cured egg yolk which makes the dish lighter yet more intensely savoury. If you haven't got the time though, just keep it traditional and crumble over a couple of hard-boiled egg yolks.

3 medium leeks
fine sea salt
2 teaspoons
  Dijon mustard
½ garlic clove,
  peeled and crushed
1 tablespoon
  white wine vinegar
1 tablespoon water
2 tablespoons
  extra virgin olive oil
2 tablespoons
  light olive oil
1 Cured Egg Yolk
  (page 202)

Trim the leeks, keeping the roots intact. Remove the green tops and any tough outer leaves, then wash thoroughly.

Bring a large pan of salted water to the boil, add the leeks and boil for 7–8 minutes until tender; the tip of a small, sharp knife should slide in easily.

Carefully remove the leeks from the pan with a skimmer or slotted spoon and pat dry with kitchen paper. Cut the leeks in half lengthways and arrange on a serving plate.

Put the mustard, garlic, vinegar and water in a bowl and whisk together until combined, then gradually whisk in the oils until the dressing has emulsified and thickened. Season to taste with salt. Spoon the dressing over the leeks, using the back of the spoon to spread it out. Finely grate the cured egg yolk over the leeks and serve.

Kimchi Bravas

I always used to be of the opinion that you shouldn't mess with classic dishes, particularly something as iconic as patatas bravas. However, times change and these are bloody delicious, so I'm happy to ignore my former self. The sauce for any good bravas, Korean-inspired or otherwise, should be deep red and sticky enough to cling to the crisp exterior of the potatoes. Toss them together moments before serving so they're coated in the sauce but still stay crispy underneath.

150ml olive oil
fine sea salt
750g Désirée potatoes, peeled and cut into roughly 3cm dice

FOR THE SAUCE:
250g kimchi
250g passata

FOR THE AIOLI:
1 medium egg yolk
2 teaspoons gochujang (Korean hot red chilli paste)
1 small garlic clove, peeled and crushed
100ml vegetable oil
2 teaspoons toasted sesame oil
1 teaspoon rice vinegar

Preheat the oven to 200°C/gas mark 6. Pour the olive oil into a roasting tin and put it into the oven to heat.

Meanwhile, bring a large pan of salted water to the boil, add the diced potatoes and boil for 10 minutes, then drain thoroughly. Tip the potatoes into the roasting tin, toss to coat in the hot oil and roast for 25 minutes until golden and crisp, tossing occasionally in the oil.

Meanwhile, for the sauce, put the kimchi and passata in a liquidiser and blend until they form a coarse paste. Pour into a saucepan, bring to a simmer and cook for 15 minutes, stirring occasionally. Remove the pan from the heat.

For the aioli, put the egg yolk, gochujang and garlic in a large bowl and whisk together until smooth. Combine the oils in a jug and, whisking constantly, begin to pour the blended oil into the bowl in a very thin, steady stream. Continue steadily adding the oil and whisking until it's all incorporated, then whisk in the vinegar.

Remove the roasting tin from the oven, lift the potatoes from the tin with a slotted spoon and briefly drain on kitchen paper. Tip the potatoes into a bowl, add half of the sauce and quickly toss to coat. Spoon the remaining sauce into a serving dish, top with the potatoes and spoon over the aioli.

Imam Bayildi with Spiced Yogurt

SERVES 4

This dish hails from Turkey and the name literally translates as 'The Imam fainted'. As with so many traditional dishes steeped in history, the origins of the name are up for discussion. I like the simple version; that the Turkish holy man fainted with pleasure at the sheer deliciousness of the dish. If you have the time, this is a dish best made a day ahead and reheated gently before serving; the flavours will develop overnight and the aubergines will soak up the rich tomato sauce.

4 aubergines
sea salt
extra virgin olive oil
1 onion, peeled and
  thinly sliced
4 garlic cloves, peeled
  and thinly sliced
2 teaspoons
  cumin seeds,
  lightly crushed
1 teaspoon
  ground coriander
½ teaspoon
  ground turmeric
1 tablespoon
  tomato purée
400g can cherry
  tomatoes
2 teaspoons
  red wine vinegar
1 teaspoon caster sugar
1 small bunch of flat-leaf
  parsley, leaves only,
  finely chopped

FOR THE SPICED YOGURT:
1 teaspoon
  ground cumin
½ teaspoon hot
  smoked paprika
¼ teaspoon
  ground turmeric
6 tablespoons thick
  Greek yogurt
squeeze of lemon juice

warm flatbreads,
  to serve

Preheat the oven to 200°C/gas mark 6. Using a small, sharp knife, cut six shallow slits along the length of each aubergine, finishing a couple of centimetres short of the base. Rub the aubergines with a generous pinch of salt, ensuring that it finds its way into the slits. As the aubergines roast, the salt will start to draw out their liquid, intensifying the flavour. Lay on a baking tray and roast for 20 minutes, turning halfway through. Transfer to a wire rack and set over the sink to allow the liquid to drain away.

While the aubergines are roasting, make the sauce. Heat a generous glug of oil – about 3 tablespoons – in a saucepan, add the onion and fry gently for 15 minutes until softened and caramelised. Add the garlic and fry for a further 5 minutes. Increase the heat slightly, add the spices and fry, stirring, for a minute until fragrant. Add a splash of water to cool the pan slightly and stop the spices from burning, then stir in the tomato purée and cook for a minute. Add the tomatoes, vinegar and sugar, bring to a simmer and cook gently for 20 minutes.

Reduce the oven temperature to 180°C/gas mark 4. Spoon a quarter of the sauce into an ovenproof dish, then lay the aubergines on top. Use a spoon to carefully open the top slit in each aubergine and create a pocket inside, then spoon the remaining sauce into the aubergines. Bake for 25 minutes. Remove from the oven and leave to cool. If you're making the dish ahead of time, leave it to cool completely, then cover and chill in the fridge.

For the spiced yogurt, add the ground spices to a small, dry frying pan and lightly toast over a medium heat for 2–3 minutes until fragrant. Tip into a bowl and stir in the yogurt, lemon juice and a drizzle of extra virgin olive oil. Season with a pinch of salt.

Sprinkle the parsley over the aubergines and serve with the spiced yogurt and warm flatbreads for mopping up.

Chickpeas with Black Kale, Rosemary and Chilli

SERVES 4

I regularly make this as a side to simple grilled or roast chicken. It's one of those great 'no thinking' dishes that requires very little effort, is ready in a flash but really delivers on flavour; perfect for a speedy dinner. Try to find the Spanish chickpeas in jars as they taste so much better than the canned varieties and have a wonderful creamy texture. Most recipes call for chickpeas to be drained and rinsed, but if they're good quality I just tip the whole jar straight in; the liquid they're kept in is full of flavour and adds body to the finished dish.

splash of olive oil
2 garlic cloves,
   peeled and crushed
½ teaspoon dried
   chilli flakes
4 sprigs of rosemary,
   leaves picked and
   chopped
4 plum tomatoes,
   deseeded and diced
660g jar chickpeas
150ml Vegetable Stock
   (page 200)
200g cavolo nero
   (black kale)

Heat the olive oil in a heavy-based pan, add the garlic, chilli flakes and rosemary and fry gently for a couple of minutes. Stir in the tomatoes and cook for 3–4 minutes until the tomatoes start to break down. Tip in the chickpeas with their liquid from the jar and the stock, bring to a simmer and cook gently for 5 minutes.

Meanwhile, remove the stalks from the cavolo nero. The easiest way to do this is to grip the thickest part of the stalk in one hand, and grab the leaf in the other hand. Sharply pull away in a straight line and the stalk should come out in one go. Discard the stalks.

Roughly tear or chop the cavolo nero leaves and add to the pan. Stir everything together and cook for 3–4 minutes until they have wilted. Pour into a warmed bowl and serve.

NOTE: You can add extra stock to this and turn it into a hearty soup.

Pommes Dauphines with Black Truffle

SERVES 4

These are seriously old-school delicious; light potato mixed with choux pastry, deep-fried until golden and crisp. Far be it for me to mess with a French classic, but they're usually served as a side dish, and I'm never really sure what to serve them on the side of. So I like to serve a big bowl of them, piping hot and covered in grated fresh truffle and sea salt. Add a chilled glass of white Burgundy and you'll have a new-found love for the potato.

500g floury potatoes,
  peeled and quartered
100ml water
75g salted butter
125g plain flour
4 medium eggs,
  beaten
sea salt
vegetable oil,
  for deep-frying
small chunk of
  Parmesan
1 small fresh black
  truffle, to serve

Put the potatoes into a large pan, cover with cold water and bring to a simmer. Cook for 25 minutes until tender, then drain thoroughly. Arrange in a single layer on a wire rack and leave to steam for 10 minutes. Pass the potatoes through a potato ricer or coarse sieve onto a baking tray, then shake to form an even layer.

While the potatoes are cooling, make the choux pastry. Heat the water and butter in a saucepan until the butter has melted, then bring to the boil. Tip the flour in all at once and beat vigorously with a wooden spoon until smooth. Continue to beat over a high heat until the mixture thickens and starts to pull away cleanly from the sides of the pan. Remove the pan from the heat and leave to cool slightly, then gradually beat in the eggs until smooth and silky. Fold in the mashed potato and season to taste with salt. Spoon the potato mixture into a piping bag fitted with a 1.5cm star nozzle.

Heat the vegetable oil for deep-frying in a large pan to 180°C. Dip the tip of a pair of kitchen scissors into the hot oil, then use to snip the potato mixture into short lengths as you pipe it straight into the oil; if you've ever made churros, you will be familiar with this technique. Deep-fry, in batches, for 2–3 minutes until golden and puffed up, then drain on a couple of plates lined with kitchen paper and season straight away with salt. Pile onto a serving platter, grate over a little Parmesan and go to town with the fresh truffle – there's no such thing as too much.

NOTE: If you want to make these without splashing out, serve them with a simple soured cream and herb dip or a mayonnaise flavoured with harissa or roast garlic.

IMAGE SHOWN ON PREVIOUS PAGE

Braised Fennel with Pangrattato

SERVES 4–6

This is one of those recipes where the flavour far outweighs the effort you have to put in. I often make this on a Sunday afternoon to go with a roast dinner and love the sweet, aniseed aroma that slowly fills the kitchen. Browning the fennel at the start of cooking is really important, as this is where you'll lay the foundations of flavour in the finished dish.

splash of olive oil
25g butter
4 medium fennel bulbs,
  halved lengthways
1 teaspoon light brown
  soft sugar
150ml Vegetable Stock
  (page 200)
dash of dry vermouth
  or dry white wine

FOR THE PANGRATTATO:
50g sourdough
  breadcrumbs
1 tablespoon olive oil
2 sprigs of rosemary,
  leaves picked and
  finely chopped
1 garlic clove, peeled
  and crushed
pinch of dried chilli flakes
pinch of sea salt

Preheat the oven to 180°C/gas mark 4. Heat the oil and butter in a heavy-based, flameproof casserole over a medium heat. Add the fennel halves, cut-side down, and fry for 10 minutes until they have turned a deep golden brown. Carefully turn them over, add the sugar, stock and vermouth or wine and bring to a simmer. Cover the pan and cook gently for 30–40 minutes until the liquid has reduced to a couple of sticky spoonfuls.

Meanwhile, put the ingredients for the pangrattato in a food processor and blend for a minute until well combined. Tip onto a baking tray and bake for 10–12 minutes until golden and crisp, stirring halfway through cooking.

Arrange the fennel on a serving plate and sprinkle over the pangrattato.

Cauliflower Cheese

Cauliflower cheese is a childhood favourite of mine, and as such is the perfect comfort food. My version makes it into more of a centrepiece by roasting the cauliflower whole, leaves and all. It intensifies the flavour of the cauliflower and means you can serve up thick wedges, dripping with cheese sauce.

1 cauliflower, with leaves, damaged or tough outer leaves removed
2 tablespoons extra virgin olive oil
sea salt

FOR THE CHEESE SAUCE:
800ml whole milk
150ml double cream
1 small onion, peeled and halved
½ teaspoon black peppercorns
1 fresh bay leaf
whole nutmeg, for grating
75g butter
75g plain flour
125g mature Cheddar, grated
30g Parmesan, finely grated

Preheat the oven to 220°C/gas mark 7. Trim the base of the cauliflower so that it sits flat, then place it in a large ovenproof dish, ensuring that the dish has sides high enough to accommodate the cheese sauce that will be added later. Brush with the olive oil, season with salt and roast for 45 minutes–1 hour, depending on the size of the cauliflower. To test if it's cooked, insert a small, sharp knife – it should slide all the way to the centre of the cauliflower with little resistance.

Meanwhile, make the cheese sauce. Put the milk, cream, onion, peppercorns and bay leaf in a saucepan and grate over plenty of nutmeg. Bring to a simmer, then remove the pan from the heat and leave to infuse for 30 minutes. Strain the liquid through a sieve into a jug, then wipe the pan clean.

Melt the butter in the same pan, add the flour and cook, stirring, for a couple of minutes until the mixture smells nutty. Gradually whisk in the infused creamy milk, a little at a time, until you have a smooth sauce. Simmer gently, stirring regularly, for 10–15 minutes until the sauce is thickened and silky. Remove the pan from the heat and stir in the Cheddar until it has completely melted. Season to taste with salt.

Remove the baking dish from the oven, lift out the cauliflower and pour in a layer of the sauce. Set the cauliflower back in the middle of the dish, then pour the remaining sauce over the top so that the whole cauliflower is coated in the sauce. Sprinkle over the Parmesan, then bake for a further 15 minutes until the top is golden brown and bubbling.

To serve, cut the cauliflower into wedges and ensure that everyone gets their fair share of the cheese sauce.

SERVES 4

Shallot Gratin

This take on a potato dauphinoise is rich, creamy and indulgent, proving that eating vegetables doesn't mean you have to be virtuous. Make sure that you really take the time to colour the shallots in the pan first to harness their intense, sweet flavour. I know this is a book all about vegetables, but this is also delicious alongside a good steak or rare roast beef.

splash of olive oil
knob of butter, plus
  extra for greasing
400g banana shallots,
  peeled and halved
  lengthways
250ml double cream
150ml whole milk
1 garlic clove, peeled
  and crushed
2 sprigs of thyme
1 fresh bay leaf
sea salt
60g Gruyère, grated

Preheat the oven to 160°C/gas mark 3. Heat the oil and butter in a heavy-based pan over a medium heat, add the shallots, cut-side down, and cook gently without disturbing for about 10 minutes until the edges are starting to turn a deep golden brown. Carefully lift one to check; the whole underside should be a deep caramel colour and should lift easily from the pan. If they're not quite there, give them a few minutes longer, but do keep an eye on them, otherwise if they burn the whole dish may taste bitter. Flip the shallots, remove the pan from the heat and leave to sit for 5 minutes.

Meanwhile, combine the cream, milk, garlic, thyme and bay leaf in a saucepan and season with plenty of salt. Bring to a simmer, then cook gently over a low heat for 10 minutes.

Grease a shallow gratin dish and arrange the shallots, cut-side up, in an even layer. Remove the thyme and bay leaf from the cream mixture, then pour it over the shallots. Scatter over the Gruyère and bake for 20 minutes until the cheese is bubbling. Remove from the oven and leave to stand for 5 minutes before serving.

Roast Jerusalem Artichokes with Sheep's Cheese and Almonds

SERVES 4

The Jerusalem artichoke, or sunchoke, is in fact not an artichoke at all, but rather the tuber of a variety of sunflower. As such, they're far easier to prepare than the globe variety, and work in much the same way as other root vegetables. Their earthy, nutty flavour is really enhanced when they're roasted until crisp and golden.

3 tablespoons olive oil
2 tablespoons honey
juice of ½ lemon
sea salt and freshly
  ground black pepper
500g Jerusalem
  artichokes, scrubbed
3 sprigs of thyme
50g flaked almonds
125g mature sheep's
  cheese, such as
  Berkswell

Preheat the oven to 200°C/gas mark 6. Whisk together the olive oil, honey, lemon juice and a good pinch of salt and black pepper in a large bowl. Slice the artichokes in half lengthways, add to the bowl with the thyme and toss to coat.

Tip the contents of the bowl into a roasting tray and arrange the artichokes, cut-side up, in an even layer. Roast for 25 minutes until the artichokes are soft on the inside and golden brown and crisp on the outside. Scatter over the flaked almonds and roast for a further 5 minutes until they are golden.

Spoon onto a warmed serving plate, crumble the cheese over the top and serve.

Roast Celery Hearts with Pecorino Cream

SERVES 4–6

Celery is used as the base of so many sauces, stock and soups but is rarely given the chance to be the main event. When celery is roasted it turns soft and sweet, transforming it completely. Make sure that you pick fresh, firm heads of celery so that they retain a little crunch at the end of cooking.

2 heads of celery
splash of olive oil
50g butter
1 tablespoon plain flour
100ml dry white wine
150ml double cream
75g pecorino,
  finely grated,
  plus extra to finish
sea salt and
  white pepper

Preheat the oven to 200°C/gas mark 6. Cut the top third off both heads of celery, finely chop the trimmings and set aside. Cut the celery hearts in half lengthways. Heat the oil and butter in a heavy-based pan over a medium heat, add the celery halves and fry for 10 minutes until golden, carefully turning occasionally.

Transfer to a baking tray and roast for 30 minutes until golden brown and tender.

Meanwhile, add the celery trimmings to the frying pan and fry over a medium heat for 10 minutes until soft. Stir in the flour and cook for a couple of minutes, then pour in the wine. Bring to the boil, then simmer for 5 minutes. Pour in the cream, bring back to the boil then simmer for a few minutes until reduced slightly. Pour into a liquidiser, add the pecorino and blend until smooth.

Transfer the roast celery to an ovenproof serving dish, pour the cream mixture over the top and scatter over a little more pecorino. Bake for 10–15 minutes until the cheesy sauce is bubbling, then serve.

Chargrilled Leeks with Romesco Sauce

SERVES 4–6

Leeks lend themselves well to a bit of heat and can take some pretty fierce charring without tasting bitter. Try to find leeks that aren't too thick – roughly 3cm is ideal – so that they cook all the way through. If your leeks are thicker, slice them in half lengthways and just be a little more careful when turning them as they can start to fall apart. Any leftover romesco sauce works well with pretty much any roast or grilled vegetables or spooned over crispy roast potatoes.

8 thin leeks
olive oil, for brushing
sea salt and freshly
    ground black pepper

FOR THE ROMESCO SAUCE:
2 dried Spanish Ñora
    peppers
2 ripe tomatoes
50g toasted flaked
    almonds
1 garlic clove, peeled
    and crushed
3–4 tablespoons extra
    virgin olive oil
1 jarred roasted red
    pepper, drained
1 slice of white bread,
    crusts removed,
    torn into chunks
sherry vinegar, to taste

First make the romesco sauce. Remove and discard the seeds from the dried peppers, then put the peppers in a small heatproof bowl, pour over boiling water to cover and leave to soak for 1 hour.

Meanwhile, preheat a cast-iron griddle pan over a high heat, then chargrill the tomatoes for 5 minutes, turning regularly until blackened and blistered all over. Remove from the pan and leave until cool enough to handle. Discard any particularly charred bits of tomato skin, then roughly chop the tomatoes.

Put the almonds, garlic and oil in a food processor and blend until smooth. Drain the soaked dried peppers, add to the food processor with the tomatoes, roasted red pepper and bread and blend to a rough paste. Season with salt and add the vinegar to taste. Set aside.

Trim the leeks, keeping the roots intact. Remove the green tops and any tough outer leaves, then wash thoroughly and pat dry with kitchen paper. Brush with olive oil and season with salt and black pepper. Reheat the griddle pan over a high heat, then chargrill the leeks, turning regularly, for 10–12 minutes until deeply charred and softened. Remove from the pan, wrap in foil and leave to steam for 5 minutes.

Arrange the leeks on a serving plate, spoon over the romesco sauce and serve.

Salt-baked Celeriac

Salt-baking is a great way of cooking root vegetables. It steams and seasons at the same time and, most importantly, all of the flavour is trapped inside while the celeriac cooks in the crust. Dukkah is an Egyptian spice and nut blend used on roasted vegetables, fish and meat. My version uses pistachios, which work beautifully with the earthy celeriac and sweet roasted lemon dressing.

400g plain flour,
  plus extra for dusting
200g fine sea salt
6 medium egg whites
3 tablespoons
  warm water
1 celeriac (about
  900g–1kg), unpeeled

FOR THE DRESSING:
1 unwaxed lemon,
  halved
2 tablespoons
  extra virgin olive oil,
  plus extra for drizzling
1 tablespoon water
1 teaspoon Dijon
  mustard
pinch of sea salt

FOR THE DUKKAH:
40g shelled
  pistachio nuts
2 teaspoons
  cumin seeds
2 teaspoons
  coriander seeds
2 teaspoons
  fennel seeds
2 teaspoons
  sesame seeds
½ teaspoon
  sea salt flakes

Preheat the oven to 160°C/gas mark 3. Put the flour and salt in a large bowl and make a well in the centre. Pour the egg whites and warm water into the well and gradually mix into the flour to form a smooth dough. Turn out onto a work surface and knead into a ball.

Dust the work surface with flour, then roll out the dough into a large round about 1cm thick. Wrap the dough around the celeriac, ensuring that there are no tears or holes, then pinch the gathered edges together to seal. Lay the wrapped celeriac on a baking tray, sealed-side down, and bake for 1½ hours. Drizzle the lemon halves with a little olive oil, add to the tray, cut-side up, and roast for a further hour. Remove from the oven and leave the celeriac to stand for 15 minutes.

Meanwhile, spread out all the ingredients for the dukkah, except the salt, on a separate baking tray and roast for 10 minutes. Remove from the oven and leave to cool slightly, then grind to a coarse powder with a pestle and mortar. Stir in the salt and set aside.

Once the lemon is cool enough to handle, remove the pips and then finely chop the skin and flesh to make the dressing. Pour over 2 tablespoons of olive oil and mash everything together to make a paste. Scrape the paste into a sieve and use the back of a spoon to press out the liquid into a large bowl. Whisk in the water and mustard, then season to taste with the salt.

Crack the salt pastry crust around the celeriac and carefully peel it away. Slice the celeriac into wedges, arrange on a warmed serving plate and drizzle over the dressing. Sprinkle over some of the dukkah and serve.

NOTE: This recipe makes more dukkah than is needed, but that's no bad thing. Keep any leftovers in an airtight container in a cool, dark cupboard. Serve it with warm flatbreads and good olive oil for dipping, or sprinkle over Hummus (see page 35) to add extra flavour and texture. It'll last for a week; any longer and the flavours start to dull.

IMAGE SHOWN ON OVERLEAF

LEAVES
& BIG
SALADS

Grilled Corn Salad with Feta and Burnt Chilli Dressing

**SERVES 4
AS A MAIN
OR SERVES 6
AS A SIDE**

Often when I'm making a roast chilli salsa to serve with Mexican dishes, I'll throw in a handful of grilled sweetcorn kernels, shaved straight off the cob into the bowl. This recipe takes it a step further to create a bold, fiery salad full of contrasting textures. The key is to add the popcorn just before serving so that it stays crisp.

olive oil
40g popping corn
sea salt
1 teaspoon hot smoked
  paprika
4 corn on the cob,
  husks and silky fibres
  removed
100g feta, crumbled
2 avocados, stoned,
  peeled and diced
1 small bunch of mint,
  leaves picked and torn

**FOR THE BURNT CHILLI
DRESSING:**
2 garlic cloves, unpeeled
2 red chillies
3 tablespoons extra
  virgin olive oil
juice of 2 limes

Heat 1 tablespoon olive oil in a large pan over a high heat, add the popping corn and immediately cover the pan. Fairly soon the corn will start popping rapidly, and as soon as the popping slows, remove the pan from the heat and set aside until the popping stops altogether. Tip the popcorn into a bowl, discarding any unpopped kernels, then season to taste straight away with salt and the paprika. Set aside.

For the dressing, heat a cast-iron griddle pan over a high heat, add the garlic and the whole red chillies and chargrill, turning occasionally, for 5 minutes until lightly charred. Remove from the pan and leave until cool enough to handle, then peel the garlic cloves and roughly chop the chillies. Put them in a small food processor with the olive oil, lime juice and a pinch of salt and blend until smooth.

Preheat a griddle pan over a high heat. Rub the corn cobs with a little olive oil and season with salt, then chargrill, turning regularly, for 8–10 minutes until softened and charred. Stand each cob in turn upright on a chopping board and use a sharp knife to slice down the length of the cob to remove the kernels. Transfer the kernels to a large bowl, add the dressing and toss to coat, then gently toss through the feta, avocado and mint. Just before serving, toss through the popcorn.

Seared Baby Gem with Black Sesame Dressing

SERVES 4–6

I can't get enough of cooked lettuce; whether it's braised with spring vegetables, cooked over hot coals, or seared as in this recipe. Adding heat completely transforms what can otherwise be a fairly plain ingredient. This dish is a real crowd-pleaser and is easy to scale up. If you're making a larger quantity of the dressing, use a food processor or high-powered 'bullet'-style liquidiser to save yourself some work when grinding the sesame seeds.

4 Baby Gem or
  Ruby Gem lettuces,
  or a mixture of both
olive oil, for brushing

FOR THE DRESSING:
6 tablespoons black
  sesame seeds
1 small garlic clove,
  peeled and crushed
2–3 tablespoons
  olive oil
1½ tablespoons
  rice vinegar
1 tablespoon dark
  soy sauce

First make the dressing. Put the sesame seeds in a small, dry frying pan and toast over a medium heat for a few minutes until starting to pop, shaking the pan frequently. Using a pestle and mortar, grind the sesame seeds to a fine paste. Add the garlic and pound until smooth, then gradually work in the olive oil until you have a smooth paste. Stir in the vinegar and soy sauce. Set aside.

Preheat a cast-iron or heavy-based stainless steel frying pan over a high heat. Halve the lettuces lengthways, keeping the roots intact, and brush with olive oil. Sear for 2 minutes on the cut side, then transfer to a warmed serving platter; depending on the size of your pan, you may need to do this in batches. Drizzle over the dressing and serve warm.

Marinated Tomatoes with Mozzarella and Basil

**SERVES 4
AS A STARTER
OR SIDE**

This is my version of the classic *Insalata Caprese*; a dish of beautiful simplicity that relies on just three top-quality ingredients. Too often you'll find this as a starter in restaurants and it's completely tasteless; bland, cheap mozzarella and flavourless, underripe tomatoes are always to blame. This version is a little more involved but really lifts the three flavours of tomato, cheese and basil to another level.

500g mixed cherry
  tomatoes
2 tablespoons
  extra virgin olive oil,
  plus extra to finish
1 tablespoon
  sherry vinegar
1 garlic clove, peeled
  and bashed
1 small bunch of
  green basil
1 small bunch of
  purple basil
pinch of sea salt
2 balls of buffalo
  mozzarella, torn

Start by preparing the tomatoes the night before. Prick each tomato with the tip of a knife, put in a heatproof bowl and pour over enough boiling water to cover. Leave to stand for 30 seconds, then drain and refresh under cold running water. Slip the skins off the tomatoes and discard.

Whisk together the olive oil and vinegar in a bowl, then add the garlic. Roughly tear half the basils and add to the bowl with the salt. Add the tomatoes and toss to combine, then cover and chill in the fridge overnight. If you're a night owl like me, pop back to the fridge and give the bowl a good shake to mix again before you go to bed.

The next day, drain the tomatoes (discarding the juices) and discard the garlic and basil; they've done their work now. Leave the tomatoes to come up to room temperature, then dress with a little more olive oil. Add the torn mozzarella and remaining basil leaves and toss to combine, then pile onto a serving plate.

Chargrilled Broccoli with Miso Dressing and Hazelnuts

**SERVES 4
AS A SIDE**

This is easily one of my favourite vegetable dishes and really epitomises my increasing love of vegetables; I would never have thought I could get excited about broccoli! Make sure that you prepare the dressing first and have it waiting in a large bowl; when you mix in the hot broccoli the egg yolk will cook just enough to create a beautiful glaze. Broccoli also has a habit of cooling down quite quickly, so make this as last-minute as possible, get it on the table and get stuck in.

25g blanched hazelnuts,
   roughly crushed
500g Tenderstem
   broccoli, ends trimmed
olive oil
sea salt

FOR THE DRESSING:
1 medium egg yolk
1 small garlic clove,
   peeled and crushed
½ teaspoon chilli powder
2 tablespoons white
   miso paste
3 tablespoons olive oil
¼ teaspoon toasted
   sesame oil
3 tablespoons
   rice vinegar

Preheat the oven to 180°C/gas mark 4. Tip the hazelnuts onto a baking tray and roast for 4–5 minutes until golden, giving them a shake halfway through cooking. Remove from the oven and leave to cool.

For the dressing, whisk together the egg yolk, garlic, chilli powder and miso paste in a large bowl. Gradually whisk in the oils, then whisk in the vinegar. Set aside.

Preheat a cast-iron griddle pan over a high heat. Toss the broccoli in a little olive oil and season lightly with salt. Add to the hot griddle pan and cook for 5 minutes until charred, turning regularly.

Transfer the chargrilled broccoli straight to the bowl of dressing and toss to coat. Spread out on a large serving plate, scatter over the roasted hazelnuts and serve.

IMAGE SHOWN OVERLEAF

SERVES 4–6

Bhel Puri

Of all the *chaat* (savoury snacks) I tried in India this was the most memorable. Possibly because of the enormous range of flavours and textures that you get in one mouthful, but also because it was so fresh and vibrant; a welcome break from all the (still delicious) fried street food we'd been eating. You can prepare all of the component parts well in advance, but don't assemble it until the very last minute, otherwise the puffed rice and sev will turn soggy. Traditionally this contains chopped boiled potato, but I prefer mine without.

2 red onions, peeled and finely chopped
2 large tomatoes, chopped
1 cucumber, deseeded and finely chopped
3 green chillies, finely chopped
2 teaspoons chaat masala
150g Indian puffed rice
150g sev
100g roasted peanuts
8 papdi, broken into small pieces
1 small bunch of coriander, leaves picked and roughly chopped
tamarind sauce, to taste

FOR THE MINT AND CORIANDER CHUTNEY:
1 small bunch of mint, leaves picked
1 small bunch of coriander
1 green chilli, chopped
20g piece of fresh ginger, peeled and grated
juice of ½ lemon
pinch of ground cumin
pinch of sea salt

Mix together the onions, tomatoes, cucumber, chillies and chaat masala in a large bowl and set aside.

Put all the ingredients for the chutney in a small food processor and blend to a smooth purée.

When you're ready to serve, add the puffed rice, sev, peanuts, papdi and coriander to the bowl of vegetables and toss to combine. Add tamarind sauce and the chutney to taste and serve immediately.

NOTE: Chaat masala, puffed rice, sev and papdi are all very common ingredients in Indian cooking, so any specialist Indian food shop will sell these.

Seared Hispi Cabbage with Brown Butter Dressing

**SERVES 4
AS A SIDE**

This recipe proves that cabbage needn't be boring. By cooking them on one side over a high heat, then letting them steam to soften, the result is something pretty special. It takes a bit of getting used to cooking vegetables using this method, as we're a nation of prodders and pokers when it comes to cooking, but the key is to leave them and not shake the pan. The cabbages should be such a deep brown that they almost look burnt, but don't worry, they won't taste bitter. If you haven't the time or inclination to make the brown butter for the dressing, just use normal butter softened at room temperature.

2 small, tight Hispi
  (pointed) cabbages
olive oil, for brushing
2 tablespoons Brown
  Butter (page 205),
  melted
1 tablespoon
  sherry vinegar
1 teaspoon
  Dijon mustard
sea salt

Heat a stainless steel or cast-iron frying pan over a medium heat. Trim away any loose outer leaves from the cabbages, then slice each in half lengthways. Brush the cut sides with olive oil, lay in the pan, cut-side down, and fry for 7–8 minutes until the cut sides have turned a deep caramel colour.

Cover the cabbages with a slightly smaller metal lid and press down firmly, then remove the pan from the heat and set aside to steam for 3–4 minutes. Test the cabbages by inserting a small, sharp knife into the thickest part – it should slide in easily.

Meanwhile, whisk together the brown butter, vinegar and mustard and season to taste with sea salt.

Arrange the cabbage on a warmed serving plate and spoon over the dressing.

Malted Root Vegetables with Barley

**SERVES 6
AS A SIDE**

I only recently discovered malt extract when we were filming some baking recipes; it was being used to great effect in a chocolate cake. However, after a bit of experimentation, it turns out that it works beautifully with vegetables in place of honey, and creates a deep, richly-flavoured glaze. It's available in most supermarkets and health food shops, so is relatively easy to source; if you really struggle to find it then go for a dark chestnut honey in its place.

100g pearl barley or farro
4 orange carrots,
  scrubbed
4 purple carrots,
  scrubbed
3 medium beetroot,
  scrubbed
4 baby parsnips
  or 2 large parsnips,
  scrubbed
3 tablespoons olive oil
3 tablespoons
  malt extract
2 tablespoons
  sherry vinegar
sea salt and freshly
  ground black pepper
1 garlic bulb, halved
  horizontally
3 sprigs of thyme
2 fresh bay leaves
vegetable oil,
  for deep-frying

Preheat the oven to 200°C/gas mark 6. Pour the pearl barley or farro into a small saucepan, cover with water and bring to the boil. Reduce the heat and simmer for 45 minutes until tender. Drain, spread out on a baking tray lined with kitchen paper and leave to steam and cool.

Meanwhile, cut the root vegetables into 4–5cm chunks, ensuring that all the pieces are roughly the same thickness. Whisk together the oil, malt extract, vinegar and a pinch of salt and black pepper in a large bowl, add the vegetables, garlic and herbs and toss to coat.

Tip the vegetable mixture into a large roasting tin, cover with foil and roast for 50 minutes. Remove the foil and roast for a further 30 minutes, shaking the tin occasionally, until the vegetables are sticky and caramelised. Remove from the oven and leave until the garlic is cool enough to handle.

Meanwhile, heat the vegetable oil for deep-frying in a saucepan to 180°C. Carefully add the pearl barley or farro and deep-fry for 2–3 minutes until golden and crisp. Remove from the oil and drain on kitchen paper, then season with a pinch of salt.

Discard the thyme and bay leaves from the vegetables, then squeeze the roasted garlic flesh from its skins and mix through the vegetables. Tip onto a serving platter, scatter over the crispy barley or farro and serve.

Coconut and Herb Noodle Salad

SERVES 4

This noodle salad is so quick to throw together that it's become a real staple in our house on busy days. In the time it takes to soak the noodles, you can make the dressing and prepare the vegetables, so it's on the table in only 15 minutes. This dish is based on the flavours of Thailand, so needs to have the right balance between hot, sweet, sour and salty; I like mine quite fiery as the coconut milk and cucumber help to extinguish the flames, but feel free to adjust the dressing to suit your own taste.

200g dried rice noodles
150ml coconut milk
juice of 1–2 limes,
   to taste
2 red bird's-eye chillies,
   chopped
2 tablespoons No-fish
   Sauce (page 205)
1 tablespoon palm sugar
200g mangetout, sliced
2 baby cucumbers,
   roughly peeled,
   deseeded and sliced
8 Thai shallots, peeled
   and finely sliced
1 small bunch of Thai
   basil, leaves picked
   and torn
1 small bunch of
   coriander, leaves
   picked and torn
1 small bunch of mint,
   leaves picked and torn
50g roasted salted
   peanuts, crushed

Put the noodles in a large, heatproof bowl, pour over enough boiling water to cover and leave to soak for 12 minutes until soft.

Meanwhile, in a large serving bowl, whisk together the coconut milk, lime juice, chillies, No-fish Sauce and palm sugar until the sugar has completely dissolved.

Drain the noodles, rinse under cold running water to cool and drain again. Tip into the bowl with the dressing and toss to coat. Add all the vegetables and herbs and divide between four bowls. Top with the crushed peanuts and serve.

Roast Kohlrabi and Carrots with Yogurt and Sumac

**SERVES 4
AS A SIDE**

Kohlrabi is a slightly odd-looking vegetable, and people are often unsure what to do with it. It's a brassica so you can treat it in the same way as cabbage or broccoli, but because the flesh is so firm it really lends itself to roasting. If you can't get hold of kohlrabi, try using the thick stalks from a couple of heads of broccoli; they have the same texture and a very similar flavour.

2 kohlrabi,
  cut into wedges
300g Chantenay carrots,
  scrubbed and halved
  lengthways
3 garlic cloves, unpeeled
2 tablespoons olive oil
sea salt and freshly
  ground black pepper
150ml thick Greek yogurt
1 teaspoon
  ground sumac
extra virgin olive oil,
  for drizzling

Preheat the oven to 200°C/gas mark 6. Tip the kohlrabi, carrots and garlic into a roasting tray and arrange in a single layer, drizzle with the olive oil and season with salt and freshly ground black pepper. Roast for 25–30 minutes until the vegetables are golden brown and tender, shaking the tray occasionally.

Remove from the oven and leave until the garlic cloves are cool enough to handle. Squeeze the roasted garlic flesh from its skins and mix with the yogurt in a large bowl. Add the kohlrabi and carrots and toss to coat. Tip into a warmed serving dish, then sprinkle over the sumac, drizzle with extra virgin olive oil and serve.

Spring Vegetable and Goat's Cheese Salad

SERVES 4

This is less a recipe and more about gathering up beautiful spring vegetables and turning them into something really pretty. Whilst I love making big platters and hearty dishes, there's something refreshing about taking some care and attention over something altogether more delicate. If you grow vegetables at home as I do, this salad is the perfect excuse to satisfy your impatience and pick a few things before you're really meant to. The main thing is to go for a variety of colours, textures and flavours.

FOR THE GOAT'S CHEESE CREAM:
150g soft goat's cheese
3–4 tablespoons whole milk

FOR THE DRESSING:
3 tablespoons rapeseed oil
2 tablespoons white wine vinegar
1 teaspoon Dijon mustard
sea salt and freshly ground black pepper
1 garlic clove, peeled and bashed

FOR THE SALAD:
fine sea salt
1 bunch of fine asparagus, trimmed
100g freshly podded peas
100g freshly podded broad beans, peeled
3–4 baby courgettes, shaved with a peeler or finely sliced
a handful of leafy breakfast radishes, finely sliced
2 small uncooked candy beetroot, scrubbed
2 small uncooked golden beetroot, scrubbed
1 head of radicchio, yellow dandelion or other bitter leaves, torn
Herb Oil (page 203), for drizzling

For the goat's cheese cream, whisk together the goat's cheese and milk in a bowl until smooth and creamy, then cover and chill in the fridge.

For the dressing, whisk together the oil, vinegar and mustard, season to taste with salt and black pepper, then stir in the garlic. Leave to infuse while the goat's cheese cream is chilling.

For the salad, bring a large pan of salted water to the boil, drop in the asparagus, peas and broad beans and cook for 2–3 minutes. Drain thoroughly, then plunge the vegetables into a large bowl of iced water. Drain and pat dry.

To serve, spread a little goat's cheese cream onto each serving plate, then start to build the salads. Lightly dress the vegetables (discard the bruised garlic clove) and arrange on the plates; start with the larger, more robust items and gradually work up to the more delicate leaves. Finish with a drizzle of Herb Oil and serve.

PICKLED & FERMENTED

Achard de Légumes

MAKES
APPROXIMATELY 1.2KG
OR 2 LARGE JARS

Whilst studying French at university I spent a year abroad, part of which was on the French Indian Ocean island of La Réunion. I didn't get much work done but did have a great time exploring the volcanic landscape and getting stuck into some seriously tasty Creole food. This vibrant pickled slaw was everywhere, either served as a side dish to grilled fish, or simply stuffed into a warm, crusty baguette. A word of warning: turmeric gets everywhere and can stain fingers, clothes, pets, etc, so wear a pair of gloves if you mix the vegetables by hand.

2 tablespoons olive oil
2 onions, peeled
  and finely sliced
3 garlic cloves,
  peeled and crushed
50g fresh ginger, peeled
  and finely grated
30g fresh turmeric,
  peeled and finely
  grated or 2 teaspoons
  ground turmeric
½ small white cabbage,
  cored and finely
  shredded
3 carrots, peeled
  and finely shredded
100g fine green beans,
  trimmed and finely
  shredded lengthways
3 mixed peppers,
  deseeded and finely
  sliced lengthways
2 green chillies, deseeded
  and finely sliced
2 teaspoons fine sea salt
2 teaspoons caster sugar
3 tablespoons
  white wine vinegar

Heat the olive oil in a medium frying pan, add the onions with the garlic, ginger and turmeric and fry over a low heat for 10 minutes until softened.

Meanwhile, combine all the remaining vegetables and the chillies in a large glass or ceramic bowl with the salt and sugar and knead with your hands for 5 minutes until soft. Drain off any excess liquid, then pour over the vinegar.

Add the onion mixture to the bowl and toss together, ensuring that all the ingredients are thoroughly combined and coated with the vinegar, then leave to cool completely.

Pack the mixture into two sterilised large clip-top jars and store in the fridge. The achard is ready to eat straight away, but is best after a week. It will keep, refrigerated, for up to 2 months.

**MAKES
APPROXIMATELY 1KG
OR 1 LARGE JAR**

Garden Pickles

This is my version of the classic Italian mixed pickled vegetables, *Giardiniera*. You can use pretty much any combination, just make sure that you pick bright, firm seasonal vegetables and don't use anything too soft like tomatoes or large courgettes, as they can turn a little mushy. If you prefer your pickles with a little kick, crumble a couple of dried red chillies into the jar as you pack the vegetables in.

200g baby turnips,
  peeled and halved
200g baby carrots,
  peeled and halved
100g baby red peppers,
  halved and deseeded
½ cauliflower,
  broken into florets
½ Romanesco,
  broken into florets
100g fine sea salt
750ml white
  malt vinegar
100g caster sugar

Combine all the vegetables in a large bowl, sprinkle over the salt and toss to combine. Cover and chill in the fridge for 4 hours.

Drain any excess liquid from the vegetables, then rinse under cold running water for 10 minutes and drain thoroughly. Have a taste of one of the pieces of vegetable, and if it tastes faintly salty, the pickles are ready. But if any more salty than that, the vegetables will require a little more rinsing. Drain the vegetables thoroughly, then pat dry with kitchen paper.

Pile the vegetables into a sterilised large clip-top jar just large enough to hold them (or use several smaller jars), then press down to pack them in tightly. Whisk together the vinegar and sugar until the sugar has completely dissolved, then pour over the vegetables. Press down on the vegetables to ensure that they're completely submerged, then seal and store in a cool, dry place for 3 weeks. Once opened, keep the pickles refrigerated and they will last for up to 6 months.

Derek's Aubergine Pickle

My father-in-law, Derek, is a keen gardener and I'm deeply envious of his greenhouse and vegetable patch (you can still be cool and want a vegetable patch). He's always making jams, chutneys and ice creams from his home-grown fruit and vegetables but this recipe is definitely the winner. Whilst I think it's destined to be served alongside rich, dark curries and steamed rice, it also works brilliantly with cold meats and cheeses. Traditionally you'd have to salt and rinse the aubergines before cooking, but the modern varieties we have nowadays aren't as bitter as they used to be so there's no need for any of that palaver.

FOR THE SPICE MIX:
1 tablespoon
   cumin seeds
2 teaspoons
   coriander seeds
2 teaspoons
   fennel seeds
1 teaspoon
   fenugreek seeds
2 dried red chillies
1 dried bay leaf

FOR THE PICKLE:
vegetable oil
3 large aubergines,
   cut into 2cm chunks
1 onion, peeled and
   finely chopped
3 garlic cloves,
   peeled and crushed
40g fresh ginger, peeled
   and finely grated
2 teaspoons yellow
   mustard seeds
1 teaspoon
   ground turmeric
1 teaspoon
   ground cinnamon
2 tablespoons
   tomato purée
50g tamarind block,
   soaked in 200ml
   boiling water for
   about 10 minutes
75g jaggery or
   demerara sugar
200ml distilled
   white vinegar
2 teaspoons
   fine sea salt

First make the spice mix. Add all the ingredients to a dry frying pan and toast over a medium heat for 3–4 minutes until fragrant. Remove the pan from the heat, then immediately tip the contents into a bowl to prevent them overcooking. Transfer to a spice grinder or small food processor and blend to a fine powder.

For the pickle, heat a splash of vegetable oil in a large, heavy-based stainless steel pan and fry the aubergines over a medium-high heat, in small batches, for 4–5 minutes at a time until golden, draining on kitchen paper as you go. Add a little more oil to the pan and fry the onion over a medium heat for 5 minutes until softened. Stir in the garlic and ginger and fry for a further few minutes. Add the spice mix, mustard seeds, turmeric and cinnamon and fry, stirring, for a minute, then add a splash of water to make a paste. Stir in the tomato purée, then strain the tamarind through a sieve, discard the pulp and add the liquid to the pan. Stir in the jaggery or demerara sugar.

Return the aubergines to the pan and fry everything for a couple of minutes until sticky. Add the vinegar and salt, bring to a simmer and cook gently for 20–25 minutes until thickened.

Spoon the pickle into sterilised jars and leave to cool, then seal and store in a cool, dark cupboard. The pickle will be ready to eat after a week, but will taste best after a month. Refrigerate once opened and, like any good pickle or chutney, it will last a good few months in the fridge.

Bread and Butter Pickles

**MAKES
APPROXIMATELY 700G
OR 1 LARGE JAR**

On recent trips to the States, I've seen these pickles pop up on menus and in delis on a regular basis, and after tasting them I had to work up my own recipe. Unlike gherkins which require a few weeks squirrelled away in a dark cupboard, these are ready to eat straightaway. As the name suggests, these pickles go with everything; as a side to smoky barbecued burgers and fried chicken, or stirred through potato salad for a sweet, vinegary crunch.

500g medium ridge or
  Lebanese cucumbers
1 sweet white onion,
  peeled and finely
  chopped
2 tablespoons
  sea salt flakes
250ml distilled
  white vinegar
250ml cider vinegar
250ml water
200g caster sugar
2 tablespoons
  yellow mustard seeds
6 allspice berries
2 dried red chillies

Slice the cucumbers into 3mm–thick rounds, put the cucumber slices in a bowl with the onion and salt and toss to combine. Be thorough here, ensuring that everything gets an even coating of salt. Cover the bowl with clingfilm and refrigerate for 4 hours.

Drain the cucumbers and onion in a large sieve, then rinse thoroughly under cold running water and drain again. Pat dry with kitchen paper and set aside.

Combine all the remaining ingredients in a large stainless steel pan and bring to the boil, then reduce the heat and simmer for 10 minutes. Add the cucumbers and onion and bring back to the boil, then remove the pan from the heat. Using a slotted spoon, transfer the cucumbers and onion to a sterilised large preserving jar (or a couple of smaller jars). Bring the pickling brine back to the boil, then carefully pour it over the cucumbers and onion, ensuring that they're completely covered. Seal the jar tightly. At this stage, you can leave the pickles to cool, then transfer to the fridge where they will keep for up to 3 weeks. Alternatively, if you're making a double batch, or simply want to keep the pickles longer and store them out of the fridge, then you'll need to follow the next step.

To process the pickles, stand the sealed jar (or jars) in a large pan and pour in enough hot water to cover by a few centimetres. Bring to the boil and then continue to boil for 15 minutes. Use a pair of tongs to remove the jar and leave to cool completely.

Either way, the pickles are ready to eat after a couple of days, but are at their best after about a week.

Pickled Tomatoes

When local tomatoes are at their peak they take some beating, but it's nice to make them last beyond summer to give a burst of freshness as the cold weather starts to draw in. My favourite use for these is alongside crispy, salty roast pork, their sweet sharpness a refreshing alternative to apple sauce. Or try tossing them with lentils, watercress and crumbly goat's cheese for a quick punchy salad.

300g mixed
  cherry tomatoes
fine sea salt
250ml distilled
  white vinegar
250ml water
2 tablespoons
  caster sugar

Use the tip of a small knife to pierce the skin of each tomato, then bring a stainless steel pan of salted water to the boil, add the tomatoes and blanch for 20–30 seconds until the skins visibly start to loosen. Drain the tomatoes and plunge into a bowl of iced water. Slip the skins off, then pat the tomatoes dry with kitchen paper; this will also remove the fluffy outer edge of the tomato flesh, which can turn the brine cloudy. Pack the tomatoes into a sterilised large preserving jar.

Add the vinegar, water, sugar and 2 teaspoons of fine sea salt to the same pan and bring to the boil, then reduce the heat and simmer for 5 minutes. Remove the pan from the heat and slowly pour the pickling liquid over the tomatoes. Seal the jar tightly. As with the Bread and Butter Pickles (see page 173), at this stage, you can leave the pickled tomatoes to cool, then transfer to the fridge where they will keep for a couple of weeks. However, if you want to keep them for longer and store them out of the fridge, then you'll need to follow the next step.

To process the pickled tomatoes, stand the sealed jar in a large pan and pour in enough hot water to cover by a few centimetres. Bring to the boil and then continue to boil for 15 minutes. Use a pair of tongs to remove the jar and leave to cool completely. They are ready to use straight away, but as with all things preserved, the flavour gets better over time.

MAKES APPROXIMATELY 400G

Garlic Pickle

This is actually more of a chutney than a pickle (although the lines between the two are fairly blurred). It may seem like a vast quantity of garlic, but the sweet acidity of the tamarind mellows any harshness and results in a rich, deeply savoury flavour. Use it as you would mango chutney, alongside fiery curries and fluffy white rice.

100g tamarind block
200ml boiling water
5 garlic bulbs
30g fresh ginger,
  peeled and chopped
4 tablespoons
  vegetable oil
1 tablespoon
  ground coriander
1 tablespoon
  Kashmiri chilli powder
2 teaspoons
  ground cumin
1 teaspoon
  ground fenugreek
½ teaspoon
  ground turmeric
1 tablespoon
  black mustard seeds
20 fresh curry leaves
2 teaspoons fine sea salt
pinch of caster sugar

Soak the tamarind block in the boiling water for 10 minutes, then strain through a sieve.

Meanwhile, to peel the garlic, bring a saucepan of water to the boil, break the bulbs into individual cloves and blanch them for 2 minutes. Drain, then refresh under cold running water – the skins should slip off easily. Pat the garlic cloves dry with kitchen paper and set aside.

Put a dozen of the peeled garlic cloves in a food processor with the ginger and half the vegetable oil and blend to a smooth paste. Set aside.

Add the ground spices to a small, dry frying pan and lightly toast over a medium heat for 2–3 minutes until fragrant. Tip into a small bowl and leave to cool.

Heat the remaining 2 tablespoons oil in a saucepan, add the mustard seeds and curry leaves and fry gently until they begin to crackle and pop. Add the remaining whole garlic cloves and fry gently for 3–4 minutes until golden. Add the garlic and ginger paste and fry gently, stirring regularly, for 5 minutes. Add the toasted ground spices and fry, stirring, for a minute. Stir in the tamarind pulp, salt and sugar, bring to a gentle simmer and cook for a further 10 minutes.

Remove the pan from the heat and leave the pickle to cool slightly, then pour into a sterilised jar with a clip-top lid. Seal and leave to cool completely. The pickle will be ready to use straight away, but as with all things preserved, the flavour gets better over time. Store in the fridge for up to 3 months.

White Kimchi

White kimchi is made in the same way as the more common red variety but without the chilli, giving it a cleaner, more refreshing flavour. It still has that familiar funk though and really benefits from at least a couple of weeks of fermenting.

1 head of Chinese leaf
  (cabbage)
3 tablespoons
  sea salt flakes
1 Asian pear or
  Williams pear, peeled,
  cored and grated
8 garlic cloves, peeled
  and roughly chopped
30g fresh ginger, peeled
  and roughly chopped
3 tablespoons No-fish
  Sauce (page 205)
3 tablespoons
  rice vinegar
2 tablespoons
  caster sugar
100ml water
1 mooli (daikon)
6 fat spring onions,
  green parts cut into
  3cm lengths, white
  parts finely sliced

Cut the base off the cabbage, then separate into individual leaves. Wash thoroughly, drain and chop into roughly 5cm pieces. Tip the cabbage into a large bowl and sprinkle over the salt. Cover tightly with clingfilm and give the bowl a good shake to ensure that the cabbage is evenly coated in the salt, then chill in the fridge for 4 hours.

Drain the cabbage and rinse thoroughly in cold water. You will need to rinse the cabbage at least three times to get rid of the excess salt. If you're not sure whether you've rinsed it enough, have a nibble – it should taste a little salty, but not unbearably so.

Put the pear, garlic, ginger, No-fish Sauce, vinegar and sugar in a food processor and blend to a smooth paste. Tip into a large bowl and stir in the water. Peel the mooli and cut it in half lengthways, then slice into half-moons. Add to the bowl along with the spring onions and cured cabbage. Give everything a good stir so that all the vegetables are nicely coated, then cover the bowl with clingfilm and chill in the fridge for 24 hours.

After 24 hours the kimchi is ready to eat, but will taste far better after a week or so of fermenting. So transfer the mixture to a sterilised large clip-top jar or two smaller ones, seal, refrigerate and be patient. It will keep for 3 months once opened.

**MAKES
APPROXIMATELY
1 LARGE JAR**

Marinated Feta

I love having a few assorted jars of nibbles at home as they make fridge-raiding altogether more enjoyable. These are a staple in our house through summer and beyond, usually served alongside some fat, juicy olives with cocktail sticks for pronging. The cubes of feta are also great tossed through salad or roasted in a hot oven and spread on small toasts. Any leftover oil will be full of flavour so keep it in the fridge for up to a month and use in salad dressings, tossed through pasta, or to dress grilled vegetables.

1 unwaxed lemon
400g feta
2 sprigs of rosemary,
  snipped into
  short lengths
2 teaspoons
  pink peppercorns,
  roughly crushed
generous pinch of
  dried chilli flakes
about 250–300ml
  olive oil

Using a sharp vegetable peeler, peel the lemon zest into strips, then scrape away any white pith with the side of a teaspoon; this takes a minute but is worth it to remove any potential bitterness.

Pat the feta dry using plenty of kitchen paper, then cut into roughly 3cm chunks.

Layer the feta in a sterilised large clip-top jar with the lemon peel strips, rosemary, peppercorns and chilli flakes. Pour over enough oil to completely cover, then seal. Gently rotate the jar a few times to mix; don't shake too vigorously, otherwise you will bruise the feta and the oil will turn cloudy. Transfer to the fridge and leave to marinate for a week before eating. It will keep, refrigerated, for a couple of weeks.

SWEET

Pumpkin Pie

This American classic has been a favourite of mine since childhood when my mum would use those tins of pumpkin purée to make deep, rich pies loaded with plenty of nutmeg. I've tried to stay as true as possible to her recipe, but prefer to use fresh pumpkin for a stronger flavour and more vibrant colour. My only slight tweak is to add a little almond extract to the pastry as it pairs perfectly with sweet, nutty pumpkin.

FOR THE PASTRY:
150g lightly salted
  butter, softened
50g icing sugar, sifted
300g plain flour,
  plus extra for dusting
2 medium egg yolks
¼ teaspoon
  almond extract
1 medium egg, beaten

FOR THE FILLING:
750g peeled, deseeded
  and diced pumpkin
300g golden
  caster sugar
250ml evaporated milk
2 large eggs
3 medium egg yolks
1½ teaspoons
  ground cinnamon
1½ teaspoons freshly
  grated nutmeg,
  plus extra to finish

For the pastry, put the butter and icing sugar in a large bowl and beat together with a wooden spoon until smooth. Add the flour and gently work together until the mixture starts to turn to a crumbly texture. Add the egg yolks and almond extract, then gently knead together with your hands to form a smooth ball. Pat out into a thin round, wrap in clingfilm and chill in the fridge for an hour.

Meanwhile, put the diced pumpkin into a large metal steamer basket set over a pan of boiling water, cover with a lid and steam for 20 minutes until tender. Tip out onto a tray lined with kitchen paper and leave to cool. Transfer the cooled pumpkin to a liquidiser, add the sugar, evaporated milk, whole eggs, egg yolks and spices and blend to a smooth purée. If you've got a powerful liquidiser it should do the job just fine, but if the mixture isn't silky smooth, pass it through a fine sieve after puréeing.

Preheat the oven to 180°C/gas mark 4. Lightly dust the work surface with flour, then roll the pastry out into a large round about 5mm thick. Line a deep 24cm round pie tin with the pastry, leaving a little excess hanging over the edges. Scrunch a large sheet of greaseproof paper into a ball and then unroll it and lay on top of the pastry; this eliminates any sharp edges and saves having to push the paper down, which can tear the pastry case. Fill the lined pastry case with uncooked rice, dried beans or baking beans and bake for 15 minutes. Remove the paper and rice or beans, brush the pastry with the beaten egg and bake for a further 10 minutes.

Reduce the oven temperature to 160°C/gas mark 3. Pour the pumpkin mixture into the pastry case and give it a gentle shake to even the surface. Bake for 50 minutes–1 hour until set with a slight wobble in the centre. Remove from the oven and leave to cool in the tin for 30 minutes, then turn out onto a wire rack and leave to cool completely. Finely grate a light dusting of nutmeg over the surface of the pie, then cut into slices and serve.

Strawberry and Pink Pepper Ice Cream

MAKES 800ML

Some of my fondest childhood memories are of strawberry picking with my brother and sister, applying the standard 'two for me, one for the basket rule', and this ice cream has its roots in those afternoons at pick-your-own farms. It should be made with perfectly ripe strawberries so that their sweet, floral flavour shines through and is lifted by the gentle heat of the pink peppercorns.

500ml whole milk
100ml double cream
3 tablespoons glucose
  syrup or golden syrup
2 tablespoons
  pink peppercorns
50g skimmed
  milk powder
500g ripe strawberries,
  hulled
150g caster sugar

Combine the milk, cream, glucose syrup and peppercorns in a saucepan. Set over a medium-high heat and bring almost to simmering point. Remove the pan from the heat, whisk in the milk powder and leave to cool for 1 hour.

Put the strawberries and sugar in a liquidiser and blend until smooth. Pour into a clean saucepan, bring to the boil and cook over a high heat for 5 minutes, stirring regularly to ensure that the sugar doesn't catch on the base of the pan. Remove the pan from the heat and leave to cool alongside the milk mixture.

Strain the cream mixture through a fine sieve then add the cooled strawberry mixture and stir to combine. Pour into an ice-cream maker and follow the manufacturer's instructions to churn until set. Transfer to a plastic container, cover with a lid and freeze for 2 hours or until firm. Remove from the freezer 10 minutes before serving to soften the ice cream enough to be scooped into cones or bowls.

Carrot, Apple and Ginger Frozen Yogurt

MAKES APPROXIMATELY 900ML

This is my attempt at making a slightly more virtuous form of ice cream. It's fresh and zingy from the yogurt and apple juice and has a subtle background heat from the fresh ginger. If you don't have a juicer gathering dust at the back of your cupboard, then put all of the ingredients into a liquidiser, blend until smooth then push through a fine sieve.

6–7 carrots, peeled
  and roughly chopped
2 Braeburn apples,
  cored and roughly
  chopped
50g fresh ginger,
  unpeeled
500ml natural yogurt
2 tablespoons honey

Pass the carrots, apples and ginger through a juicer – you should get just over 400ml juice.

Pour the juice into a large jug, add the yogurt and honey and stir until the honey has dissolved.

Transfer the mixture to an ice-cream maker and follow the manufacturer's instructions to churn until set. Transfer to a plastic container, cover with a lid and freeze for 1 hour until firm. Soften out of the freezer for 10 minutes before serving. This will keep in the freezer for up to 3 months.

Alternatively, if you're making this for children, reduce the amount of ginger slightly then pour into lolly moulds and freeze until firm.

Spiced Carrot Kulfi

MAKES 6–8, DEPENDING ON THE SIZE OF THE MOULDS

This combines two of my favourite sweet treats that I came to love when we visited India; masala chai and kulfi. Both tend to be made teeth-squeakingly sweet, so I've toned down the sugar slightly and have replaced the traditional saffron with grated carrot (saffron is pretty much the only flavour I really don't like).

400ml whole milk
397g can condensed milk
3 carrots, peeled and grated
4 green cardamom pods
1 black cardamom pod
1 cinnamon stick
3 cloves
50g shelled pistachio nuts, finely chopped

Combine all the ingredients, except the pistachios, in a wide, heavy-based saucepan and bring to the boil. Reduce the heat and simmer gently for 20 minutes until the carrot is completely soft. Remove the pan from the heat and leave to cool completely.

Fish out the spices and discard, then pour the milk and carrot mixture into a liquidiser and blend until smooth. Leave to cool. Once cool, pour the mixture into 6–8 ice-cream moulds and freeze for 4 hours or overnight until firm.

To serve, remove the moulds from the freezer and leave to stand for 5 minutes before turning out. Roll in the chopped pistachios and serve.

NOTE: If fishing out the spices after cooking them in the milk and carrot mixture seems like a faff, tie them up in a little muslin cloth parcel before adding to the pan to save you from hunting around for stray cardamom pods or cloves.

Rhubarb and Custard

MAKES
APPROXIMATELY
1.2 LITRES

This recipe is pure nostalgia as it taps into so many of my food memories. I still love those little boiled sweets, one half bright yellow, the other a shocking pink, both sweet and sour at the same time. The nutmeg in the custard gives it the flavour of one of my favourite foods of all time – wobbly, rich custard tarts – and makes the whole thing taste even more custardy. Incidentally, rhubarb is actually a vegetable, but that was never the thinking behind the inclusion of this pudding – it's just absolutely, bowl-scrapingly delicious.

FOR THE RHUBARB SORBET:
500g trimmed pink
  rhubarb sticks,
  chopped into
  1cm lengths
250ml grenadine
50g glucose syrup or
  golden syrup

FOR THE CUSTARD ICE CREAM:
250ml whole milk
250ml whipping cream
pinch of freshly
  grated nutmeg
50g glucose syrup
4 medium egg yolks
50g caster sugar
30g skimmed
  milk powder

Combine the ingredients for the sorbet in a wide saucepan, bring to the boil and cook for 5–6 minutes until the rhubarb is just tender. Remove the pan from the heat and leave to cool slightly, then pour the contents into a liquidiser and blend until completely smooth. Pour the rhubarb mixture into a jug, cover and chill in the fridge.

For the ice cream, combine the milk, cream, nutmeg and glucose syrup in a saucepan and bring to a simmer. Meanwhile, whisk the egg yolks and sugar together in a heatproof bowl. Whisk the milk powder into the hot milk mixture, then pour over the yolks, whisking to combine. Pour the custard mixture back into the pan and heat gently, stirring constantly with a heatproof spatula or wooden spoon, until the mixture has thickened enough to coat the back of a spoon. Immediately take the pan off the heat and pass through a sieve into a clean bowl. It's crucial that you do this as soon as the custard's ready, otherwise if you leave it sitting in the pan even off the heat, the residual heat in the pan will overcook the custard and it will turn grainy. Pour the custard into a jug, cover the surface with clingfilm and leave to chill in the fridge.

Transfer the custard to an ice-cream maker and follow the manufacturer's instructions to churn until set. Put in a 2-litre plastic container, cover with a lid and place in the freezer. Churn the rhubarb sorbet mixture in the same way, and as it starts to set, take the custard out of the freezer; it should still be fairly soft. Drop spoonfuls of the sorbet onto the custard ice cream and use the tip of a butter knife to swirl the two together. Don't overdo the swirling, otherwise you will just end up with pink ice cream, which won't have the striking ripple effect. Cover and return to the freezer for at least 3 hours or overnight until firm. Remove from the freezer 10 minutes before serving to soften. It will keep in the freezer for up to 3 months.

Spiced Pumpkin Chocolate Mousse

SERVES 4

This recipe came about entirely by accident. I'd been testing the recipe for the Pumpkin Pie (page 182) and had a slice left over in the fridge. On a night time fridge-raid in search of something sweet, I took a forkful of pie and a few squares of chocolate and the rest, as they say, is history. Make sure that the pumpkin purée is completely cool before spooning the mousse on top, otherwise it'll split and you'll end up with a runny, albeit delicious, mess.

FOR THE PUMPKIN PURÉE:
650ml boiling water
300g peeled and
  deseeded pumpkin
  or butternut squash,
  coarsely grated
3 tablespoons
  caster sugar
1 vanilla pod, split
  lengthways and
  seeds scraped out
generous pinch of
  freshly grated nutmeg
½ teaspoon ground
  cinnamon

FOR THE MOUSSE:
125g dark chocolate
  (70% cocoa solids),
  broken into small
  pieces
2 large egg yolks
2 tablespoons
  boiling water
4 large egg whites
pinch of sea salt flakes
2 tablespoons
  caster sugar

2 amaretti biscuits,
  crushed, to serve

Combine all the ingredients for the pumpkin purée in a saucepan, adding the vanilla pod with the seeds, bring to the boil and cook for 8–10 minutes until the pumpkin or squash starts to fall apart. Discard the vanilla pod and leave the mixture to cool slightly, then pour it into a liquidiser and blend until smooth. Pour into a bowl and leave to cool completely.

Divide the pumpkin purée between four serving glasses or small bowls and leave to chill in the fridge while you make the mousse.

Melt the chocolate in a heatproof bowl set over a saucepan of barely simmering water. Remove the bowl from the heat, and leave the chocolate to cool slightly. Beat the egg yolks into the melted chocolate and gradually stir in the boiling water.

In a clean bowl, whisk the egg whites with the salt until soft peaks form, then gradually add the sugar and whisk until thick and shiny. Fold the whisked egg whites into the chocolate mixture, one third at a time, until completely smooth and streak-free. Carefully spoon the mousse on top of the pumpkin, then chill in the fridge for 2 hours until set.

Scatter the tops of the mousses with the crushed amaretti biscuits and serve.

White Miso Crème Brûlée

Salted caramel is a delicious flavour combination and when the balance of sweet and salty is just right it has an addictive quality. But if that salty element comes from miso you throw umami into the mix, taking that flavour combination to another level entirely. White miso has a sweetness of its own so I use a little less sugar than normal in this recipe.

80g caster sugar
600ml double cream
6 medium egg yolks
2 tablespoons white
  miso paste
3 tablespoons
  demerara sugar

Preheat the oven to 150°C/gas mark 2. Heat the sugar in a saucepan over a medium heat, without stirring, until it has melted in largish patches, only then swirling the pan to spread the molten sugar into the remaining unmelted sugar. Once all the sugar has melted and turned a deep caramel colour, pour in the cream and leave it to bubble away furiously for a minute, then remove from the heat and whisk with a balloon whisk until smooth; there should be no pieces of caramel remaining.

Whisk together the egg yolks and miso paste in a large bowl, then whisk in the hot caramel cream until smooth.

Divide the mixture between six ramekins and stand them in a roasting tin. Pour in enough boiling water to come halfway up the sides of the ramekins, and bake for 35–40 minutes until just set with a slight wobble in the centre. Carefully remove the ramekins from the roasting tin and leave to cool, then chill in the fridge for 2 hours.

Pound the demerara sugar using a pestle and mortar to a fine powder, dust over the tops of the custards and caramelise with a chef's blowtorch. Leave to cool for a few minutes and then serve.

Spiced Carrot and Fig Pudding with Bourbon

SERVES 6–8

This is based on my all-time favourite: sticky toffee pudding. It's the pudding I'll always scan a menu for and will usually judge a restaurant or pub solely on how good their version is. For it to be just right it needs to be dark, sticky and intensely sweet without being too heavy or cloying. The carrot keeps things moist and I've used figs instead of dates as I love the pop and crunch of the seeds. I love pretty much anything containing bourbon whiskey so there's plenty in the sauce, but if you want to make it booze-free you can replace it with apple juice.

120g dried figs
1 teaspoon bicarbonate of soda
250ml boiling water
2 tablespoons malt extract or dark treacle
75ml bourbon whiskey
50g lightly salted butter, plus extra for greasing
100g dark brown soft sugar
2 large eggs, beaten
100g self-raising flour, sifted
100g plain wholemeal flour
2 carrots, peeled and finely grated
2 teaspoons ground ginger
2 teaspoons ground black pepper

FOR THE SAUCE:
200g lightly salted butter
200g dark brown soft sugar
3–4 tablespoons bourbon whiskey

clotted cream, to serve

Preheat the oven to 180°C/gas mark 4 and grease a 22cm square cake tin with butter.

Remove the stems from the figs, then finely chop the flesh and tip it into a bowl. Stir in the bicarbonate of soda, pour over the boiling water and leave to stand for 10 minutes. Stir in the malt extract or dark treacle and bourbon.

Cream the butter and sugar in a bowl with a hand-held electric whisk or in a stand mixer fitted with the paddle attachment until pale and fluffy, then beat in the eggs, one at a time. Fold in the flours, grated carrots, ground ginger and black pepper, then gradually stir in the fig mixture. Pour the batter into the lined tin and bake for 30 minutes.

Meanwhile, for the sauce, heat the butter and sugar in a small saucepan for 5 minutes, stirring, until the sugar has dissolved and the mixture starts to thicken. Remove from the heat and whisk in the bourbon – take care, as the mixture will splutter.

Pour half the sauce over the top of the pudding, then bake for a further 8–10 minutes, keeping the remaining sauce warm. Remove the pudding from the oven, cut into squares and divide between serving bowls. Serve warm with the remaining sauce and a spoonful of clotted cream.

Celeriac Rice Pudding with Bramble Compote

SERVES 4

When you think of comforting autumnal puddings, I'd guess that celeriac wouldn't feature as a star ingredient. However, that sweet, earthy flavour combined with subtle spices in a classic rice pudding tastes pretty incredible. Also by making a silky smooth purée from the celeriac, the finished rice is rich and creamy, but nowhere near as heavy as when it's made with double cream. It may seem a little odd, but trust me; if you like rice pudding, you'll love this.

250g peeled celeriac, finely diced
250ml whole milk
25g caster sugar
1 vanilla pod, split lengthways and seeds scraped out
generous pinch of freshly grated nutmeg

FOR THE RICE BASE:
450ml whole milk
100g pudding rice
25g caster sugar
finely grated zest of 1 unwaxed lemon

FOR THE BRAMBLE COMPOTE:
200g blackberries
2 teaspoons caster sugar
squeeze of lemon juice

Put the celeriac, milk, sugar, vanilla seeds and pod and nutmeg in a saucepan and bring to a simmer. Cover the pan and cook for 25 minutes until the celeriac is soft; it should give easily when pressed against the side of the pan with a spoon. Discard the vanilla pod, then pour the mixture into a liquidiser and blend to a smooth purée.

Meanwhile, combine all the ingredients for the rice base in a separate saucepan, bring to a simmer and cook gently for 25 minutes, stirring occasionally.

Stir the celeriac purée into the rice and return to a simmer, then remove the pan from the heat, cover with a lid and leave to stand for 5 minutes.

Combine all the ingredients for the compote in a small saucepan, bring to a simmer and cook gently for 5 minutes – the blackberries should start to soften but still hold their shape.

Divide the rice pudding between warmed serving bowls and spoon over the compote, then serve.

Beetroot and Blackcurrant Sorbet with Salted Honeycomb

SERVES 4–6

For me, desserts are full of nostalgia and a great way to revisit early memories. There's something about sweet flavours that seems to have a stronger link to our childhood than savoury; perhaps it's because we ate such great homemade puddings growing up, but I suspect it's simply that desserts always make you happy and so forge such positive memories. This recipe does exactly that, as the flavours of blackcurrant and honeycomb played such a strong part in my early years. Whenever we went to France, my brother and I would always go for chocolate ice cream and blackcurrant sorbet in a cone, and my mum used to make incredible blackcurrant mousses for dinner parties. My dad was, and still is, a massive fan of crunchy honeycomb, which is delicious against the sweet, earthy flavour of this sorbet.

250ml beetroot juice
150g caster sugar
50g glucose syrup
500g blackcurrants, fresh or frozen

FOR THE SALTED HONEYCOMB:
100g caster sugar
2 tablespoons golden syrup
2 tablespoons honey
pinch of sea salt flakes
2 teaspoons bicarbonate of soda

Combine the beetroot juice, sugar and glucose syrup in a saucepan and heat gently until the sugar has melted, stirring. Add the blackcurrants, bring to a gentle simmer and cook for 10 minutes until softened. Strain the contents of the pan through a fine sieve, pressing down with a ladle to extract as much juice as possible, and then leave to cool.

Pour the mixture into an ice-cream maker and follow the manufacturer's instructions to churn until set. Transfer to a plastic container, cover with a lid and freeze for 2 hours or until firm.

For the salted honeycomb, line a baking tray with greaseproof paper. Heat the sugar, syrup and honey in a wide saucepan, without stirring, until the sugar has melted and starts to turn a deep caramel colour. Remove the pan from the heat, scatter over the sea salt and then stir through the bicarbonate of soda. When the mixture begins to bubble up dramatically, pour it slowly and carefully into the lined baking tray, then set aside to cool completely.

Break the honeycomb into shards and serve with scoops of the sorbet.

BASICS

Vegetable Stock

MAKES
APPROXIMATELY
2.5 LITRES

A good stock is the backbone of so many recipes and really makes a difference to the flavour of a finished dish. Unlike meat stocks, the flavour of vegetable stock can dull quite quickly. With that in mind it's always best to make it fresh, if you have time, or make a big batch and freeze it immediately.

2 tablespoons olive oil
3 medium leeks, white
   parts only, washed
   and diced
3 carrots, peeled
   and diced
2 onions, peeled
   and diced
4 closed cup white
   mushrooms, diced
1 fennel bulb, diced,
   or 1 star anise
a handful of parsley stalks
4 sprigs of thyme
1 fresh bay leaf
½ teaspoon white
   peppercorns
3 litres water

Heat the olive oil in a large stock pot, add all the vegetables and fry gently for 10 minutes until softened but not coloured. If you're using star anise rather than fennel, remove it at this point.

Add the herbs and peppercorns and then pour over the cold water. Bring to the boil, then reduce the heat and simmer for 30 minutes.

Strain the stock through a fine sieve and leave to cool, then cover and refrigerate. Use within 48 hours or freeze.

Pumpkin Stock

MAKES
APPROXIMATELY
1.5 LITRES

This is a great way to use up the seeds, pulp and trimmings that you're always left with when preparing pumpkins or squash. It's a great stock in its own right and can be used for all sorts of recipes, from soups to stews, and is the perfect base for the Butternut Squash Laksa (page 76). Just like the Vegetable Stock the flavour and colour can dull fairly quickly, so it's best to use this within a day or so and freeze any left over.

2 tablespoons olive oil
seeds, pulp and
   trimmings from
   1 pumpkin or squash
2 onions, peeled
   and diced
2 celery sticks, diced
1 star anise
2 fresh bay leaves
½ teaspoon white
   peppercorns
500ml carrot juice
1.5 litres water

Heat the olive oil in a large stock pot, add all the vegetables and the star anise and fry gently for 10 minutes until softened but not coloured.

Remove the star anise and add the bay leaves, peppercorns and carrot juice, then pour over the cold water. Bring to the boil, then reduce the heat and simmer for 30 minutes.

Strain the stock through a fine sieve and leave to cool, then cover and refrigerate. Use within 48 hours or freeze.

MAKES 4

Cured Egg Yolks

There's something incredibly satisfying about taking an ingredient as simple as an egg yolk and turning it into something really special. These semi-translucent little gems add a savoury depth and richness to dishes; I use these in the Leeks Vinaigrette recipe (page 129), but they last for a while in the fridge and are really versatile. Try finely grating over vegetables, pastas, soups or salads, just as you would with a hard cheese. I tend to use eggs from corn-fed hens as the yolks are a deep, vibrant orange and when cured their colour is further intensified.

250g fine sea salt
250g caster sugar
4 large corn-fed
  egg yolks
vegetable oil, for oiling

Put the salt and sugar in a bowl and mix together thoroughly. Tip two thirds of the mixture into a plastic container or small baking tray, then use the fatter end of an egg to press down and make four little craters. Slip an egg yolk into each and carefully cover with the remaining salt–sugar mixture. Cover the container with a tight-fitting lid or with a few layers of clingfilm, then chill in the fridge for 4 days.

Preheat the oven (or a dehydrator if you happen to have one) to 65°C. Carefully remove the egg yolks from the salt–sugar mixture and use a soft pastry brush to remove as much excess as possible. At this stage, the yolks will feel firmer and the colour will have intensified. Rinse the yolks under cold running water and gently pat dry with kitchen paper.

Lightly oil a wire rack and set it on top of a baking tray. Lay the yolks on the rack and dry out in the oven for 1½–2 hours until firm. Remove from the oven and leave to cool. Store the cured egg yolks in an airtight container in the fridge for up to 3 weeks.

NOTE: Moisture in the fridge can spoil the cured yolks, so ensure that they are kept in an airtight container. For an extra level of protection, I add a packet of silica gel to the container to help absorb any moisture (the type you get in the box when you buy a new pair of trainers or an electrical gadget).

Lemon Oil

MAKES
APPROXIMATELY
450ML

It's incredibly easy to make your own lemon oil. Make sure that you take the time to scrape away any white pith as it can leave a bitter aftertaste. I use unwaxed lemons, but regular lemons are fine if you give them a quick scrub in hot water before peeling.

3 unwaxed lemons
500ml light olive oil

Using a sharp vegetable peeler, remove the lemon peel in strips, then use a small knife to scrape away any white pith.

Put the lemon peel in a saucepan and use the end of a rolling pin to gently pound and crush until oily and fragrant.

Pour over the olive oil and warm gently over a low heat for 10 minutes, stirring occasionally. Remove the pan from the heat and leave to infuse at room temperature for 6 hours.

Strain the oil through a fine sieve and a funnel into a sterilised glass bottle, then seal. Store in a cool, dark place for up to 3 months.

Herb Oil

MAKES
APPROXIMATELY
150ML

I only ever make this in small quantities as the flavour and colour starts to dull after a few days. The key is to keep everything as vibrant as possible, so chilling in an ice bath is crucial. Just like a good extra virgin olive oil, this is an oil for finishing dishes rather than frying. Drizzle it over salads, fish or chicken, or use as the base for a light, herby vinaigrette.

fine sea salt
1 small bunch of
  flat-leaf parsley,
  roughly chopped
1 small bunch of chives,
  roughly chopped
1 small bunch of basil,
  leaves picked
1 small bunch of
  tarragon, leaves picked
1 small bunch of
  soft thyme
250ml light olive oil

Make an ice bath by half-filling a large bowl with ice and water, and set a smaller bowl inside to chill. Bring a large pan of salted water to the boil, add all the herbs and blanch for 10 seconds. Quickly drain through a sieve and refresh under cold running water.

Put the herbs and oil in a liquidiser and blend until smooth, then pour straight into the ice bath. Leave to chill for 15 minutes, stirring occasionally.

Line a sieve with a muslin cloth, then set it over a bowl or jug, pour in the herb mixture and leave to drip for 30 minutes. Don't press down on the mixture to try to force it through, as it will turn the oil cloudy. Discard any remaining herb mixture.

Pour the herb oil into a sterilised glass bottle, seal and store in the fridge. The oil will keep, refrigerated, for up to a week, and any left over will freeze well.

Chilli Oil

We have a bottle of this next to our hob on permanent rotation; when a bottle's nearly empty I get another one on the go so we don't run out. I originally made this to drizzle over pizza but now it goes on everything from fried eggs to noodles, pastas and soups. You can also use it as a base for a fiery mayonnaise or salad dressing or to add a kick to roast potatoes.

8 dried red chillies
400ml light olive oil

Preheat the oven to 160°C/gas mark 3. Prick the chillies all over with a pin or the tip of a sharp knife, then lay them on a baking tray and roast for 10 minutes.

Tip the chillies into a saucepan, pour over the oil and warm gently over a low heat for 10 minutes, stirring occasionally. Remove the pan from the heat and leave the chillies to cool in the oil.

Pick out the chillies and drop into a sterilised glass bottle. Pour the oil through a funnel into the bottle, then seal. Store in a cool, dark place for 6 months.

Mushroom Ketchup

There are two types of mushroom ketchup; the thin, spiced liquid akin to Worcestershire Sauce and the thick, rich stuff for dipping chips into. This recipe is for the latter. As with any ketchup or chutney the acidity mellows and the flavour develops over time.

250g portobello
  mushrooms, chopped
8 dried shiitake
  mushrooms, chopped
1 small onion, peeled
  and roughly chopped
1 garlic clove,
  peeled and crushed
500ml water
150ml cider vinegar
75g caster sugar
2 tablespoons
  dark soy sauce
1 star anise
2 tablespoons
  Dijon mustard

Put all the ingredients, except the star anise and mustard, in a liquidiser and blend until smooth.

Pour the mixture into a stainless steel saucepan, add the star anise and bring to the boil. Reduce the heat and simmer gently for 30 minutes, stirring occasionally. The mixture will start off quite pale, but should be rich and dark by the time it's ready.

Fish out the star anise, then pour the mixture back into the liquidiser. Add the mustard and whizz until smooth, then pour through a funnel into a sterilised glass bottle, seal and store in the fridge. The sauce will keep, refrigerated, for up to 3 months.

Brown Butter

MAKES
APPROXIMATELY
175G

The brown colour of this butter comes from the milk solids slowly caramelising as the butter cooks, so the result is a sweet, nutty liquid that can be used in all sorts of cooking. Add a spoonful to pancake batter, drizzle over fried eggs, fish or pasta. It's best to use a small stainless steel pan as the bottom isn't too dark so you'll find it easier to keep an eye on the colour of the butter as it cooks.

250g unsalted butter, diced

Line a sieve with a couple of sheets of kitchen paper or a square of muslin cloth.

Put the butter in a saucepan and set over a medium heat. Once the butter has completely melted, increase the heat and cook for 3–4 minutes, whisking constantly with a balloon whisk. The butter will quickly start to brown, so make sure you keep an eye on it. As soon as it has turned a rich brown, the colour of maple syrup, remove the pan from the heat and immediately strain through the lined sieve. Don't delay, as the residual heat in the pan will continue cooking the butter and could burn it.

Leave to cool completely, then pour into a lidded container, cover with the lid and store in the fridge. The butter will keep for up to 2 weeks.

No-fish Sauce

MAKES
APPROXIMATELY
250ML

One of the biggest challenges writing this book was Southeast Asian cuisine. I wanted to keep the flavours authentic, but fish sauce tends to crop up everywhere and has such a distinct flavour that couldn't just be omitted. It took several trials, and lots of taste tests, but I've finally cracked it. This should taste intensely savoury and very salty with just enough funk to replicate the pungency of Thai fish sauce.

20g piece of dried kombu, rinsed
4 dried shiitake mushrooms, sliced
3 tablespoons brown miso paste
2 tablespoons light soy sauce
2 tablespoons cider vinegar
1 tablespoon fine sea salt
500ml boiling water

Using a pair of kitchen scissors, cut the kombu into thin strips and put in a stainless steel saucepan. Add the remaining ingredients and bring to the boil, then simmer for about 15 minutes until reduced by half.

Remove the pan from the heat, strain the liquid through a fine sieve into a jug and leave to cool completely. Transfer to a sterilised glass bottle, seal and store in the fridge. The sauce will keep, refrigerated, for up to 4 weeks.

Index